WHAT YOU THINK YOU KNOW ABOUT FOOTBALL IS WRONG

THE GLOBAL GAME'S GREATEST MYTHS AND UNTRUTHS

Dr KEVIN MOORE

BLOOMSBURY SPORT

LONDON • OXFORD • NEW YORK • NEW DELHI • SYDNEY

BLOOMSBURY SPORT
Bloomsbury Publishing Plc
50 Bedford Square, London, WC1B 3DP, UK

BLOOMSBURY, BLOOMSBURY SPORT and the Diana logo are trademarks of
Bloomsbury Publishing Plc

First published in Great Britain 2019

Copyright © Kevin Moore, 2019

Kevin Moore has asserted his right under the Copyright, Designs and
Patents Act, 1988, to be identified as Author of this work

For legal purposes the Acknowledgements on p. 223
constitute an extension of this copyright page

All rights reserved. No part of this publication may be reproduced or transmitted in
any form or by any means, electronic or mechanical, including photocopying,
recording, or any information storage or retrieval system, without prior
permission in writing from the publishers

Bloomsbury Publishing Plc does not have any control over, or responsibility for,
any third-party websites referred to or in this book. All internet addresses given
in this book were correct at the time of going to press. The author and publisher
regret any inconvenience caused if addresses have changed or sites have ceased
to exist, but can accept no responsibility for any such changes

A catalogue record for this book is available from the British Library

Library of Congress Cataloguing-in-Publication data has been applied for

ISBN: HB: 978-1-4729-5566-1; eBook: 978-1-4729-5567-8

2 4 6 8 10 9 7 5 3 1

Typeset in Haarlemmer MT by Deanta Global Publishing Services, Chennai, India
Printed and bound in Great Britain by CPI Group (UK) Ltd., Croydon, CR0 4YY

To find out more about our authors and books visit www.bloomsbury.com
and sign up for our newsletters

CONTENTS

CONTENTS

CONTENTS

FOREWORD BY JOHN MOTSON, OBE

Over nearly 50 years of commentating on football, I've witnessed, often first-hand, many of the iconic moments in the history of the game, including Sunderland's David versus Goliath win over Leeds in the FA Cup Final, Maradona's Hand of God goal and Leicester City's incredible Premier League victory. The stories and theories that arise from such moments are forever repeated and expounded on in pubs and workplaces. They become part of the fabric of the sport; apparently reliable assertions that help us make sense of football's traditions and history.

This book takes a wrecking ball to many of the myths and assumptions about football that usually pass unchallenged. At times it left me surprised and even a little shocked. Dr Moore, who I know to be an expert on the history of football, has delved into every aspect of the game, from the accepted origins of women's football to the importance of the colour of team shirts. He has no sacred cows. Some may ask how he can question England's 1966 World Cup win or Alex Ferguson's place in the football firmament, but he does – and puts up a pretty convincing argument, too.

Those who like to debate and dispute conventional football wisdom will devour these pages filled with facts, anecdotes and analysis. And if it turns out the beautiful game isn't quite as straightforward and black and white as it's often painted, doesn't that just make it even more beautiful?

FOREWORD BY GUY MOWBRAY

A commentator's lot is not an easy one. Fall back on a truism such as, 'There are no easy games at this level' or even, 'It's a game of two halves' and you get the whole Twittersphere laughing at or taking issue with you. So, thanks a bundle Kevin Moore! The author of this tome has taken some of the dependable truths, some that even those of us steeped in football lore have taken for granted for years, and ripped them apart.

In claiming that football fans are mistaken in virtually everything we believe about football, Dr Moore is, as Sir Alex Ferguson once described Dennis Wise, a man capable of starting an argument in an empty room. Playing at home is a great advantage; Englishmen taught Brazilians to play football; Denis Law's back-heel relegated Manchester United... The author begs to differ and has the facts to back up his case.

It's a feast of contrary and controversial assertions which make you question so much you assume to be true about the game. So next time you hear a commentator remarking on the natural artistry of the Brazilian player, the emergence of the Premier League prawn sandwich brigade or the unerring club loyalty of English football fans, you'll be able to take them to task.

INTRODUCTION

We humans love myths. And we always have. And the more passionate we are about something, the more likely we are to tell – and invent – stories about it. If something didn't actually happen the way it did, we bend the truth, to make it a better story. We all do this every day. Why let the facts get in the way of a good anecdote? The more the story then gets repeated, the more likely it will be accepted as the truth – and this can happen very quickly.

Association football is only just over 150 years old, but because many of us are so passionate about it, stories, myths and legends abound, even about quite recent incidents in the game. This book debunks many of these myths. Through meticulous research, it peels back the fiction to get as close as we can to the truth. Of course it is still my interpretation, but I have set out to be as objective as I can. I believed many of these myths, so it has pained me at times to find out that they are not true! I was director of the National Football Museum for England from 1997 to 2017, establishing it first in Preston and then in Manchester, so I have spent over 20 years of my life working with football's history, including research and writing. This book comes from much that I have learned in that time.

I hope that you are intrigued and surprised at what I have found. You may at times even get a little annoyed as I debunk one of your favourite football stories or beliefs. But given our passion for the game, sometimes we have to set this aside, to understand the game as it really is.

Given how we have collectively mythologised the game so much, there are many myths I haven't included in this volume. Soldiers in the First World War *did* play football in no man's land between the trenches on Christmas Day 1914 – but the Germans won! Football is *not* the world's most popular sport. WAGs are not new in football – they have always been part of the game. The 'Hand of God' goal was fair enough – England have cheated just as much on the pitch as Argentina. Sometimes the truth hurts!

1

THE BALL *DID* CROSS THE LINE IN THE 1966 WORLD CUP FINAL – AND WE KNEW THIS IN 1966

Wembley Stadium, 30 July 1966. The World Cup Final. England against West Germany. The score is 2-2, in extra time. In the 101st minute Geoff Hurst shoots, the ball hits the bar, and … Is it a goal? For over 50 years, England's only World Cup Final win has been tarnished by accusations (mainly by Germans) that the ball was not over the line for the third England goal and it shouldn't have been given. This is nonsense. The ball did cross the line; the referee was right to give the goal.

The Swiss referee, Gottfried Dienst, wasn't quite sure at the time, as quite naturally he was behind the play. In 1966 he was considered the best referee in the world. Dienst is one of only four men to have twice refereed a European Cup final, and one of only two to have refereed both the European Championship final and the World Cup Final. He consulted his linesman from the USSR, Tofiq Bahramov, who was level with the play and who was certain it was a goal. Bahramov was also a highly experienced and very well-respected international referee. He refereed a first-round match in 1966 and three games at the 1970 World Cup finals, including a semi-final. So the highly respected linesman had no doubt. The West German TV commentary of the goal was 'Danger! Danger! Not in the goal! No goal!', but once it was given, a resigned 'Goal'. Even for those who didn't believe the ball was over the line, the referee's decision was final.

So why has there been *any* controversy? The problem is that while 96,924 people were at the game, only a few thousand of these had a clear goal line view. Most people were watching on TV – over 30 million in the UK and over 300 million worldwide. The television pictures, in grainy black and white, *are* inconclusive. But even today, television distorts events on the field of play in football and in other sports. For example, low catches in cricket. To the naked eye, they are clearly a catch. But when the umpires on the field are uncertain and refer them up to the third umpire in the stand, watching on TV, he or she will often give the decision as not out, because in the TV pictures the ball appears to touch the ground. TV distorts now – and it did so far more back in 1966. The 405-line system used then was referred to as 'high definition', but the actual image was only 377 lines high. Sir David Attenborough has reflected that 405 lines was 'dreadful quality'. BBC Two, of which Attenborough was then the controller, had 625 lines, but wasn't covering the game! ITV had the same television pictures as the BBC, but as 29 million people were watching on the BBC and only 3 million on ITV, BBC commentator Kenneth Wolstenholme's words for England's fourth goal – 'Some people are on the pitch, they think it's all over, it is now!' – have passed into history, whereas Hugh John's equally eloquent commentary on ITV – 'Here's Hurst, he might make it three. He has! He has … so that's it. That is IT!' – has been forgotten.

Image analysis of footage of the goal from two angles by engineering scientists at the University of Oxford in 1995 concluded that the ball did not fully cross the line – it was six centimetres short. However, this was flawed by being based on the 405-line black-and-white TV pictures. Other subsequent German analyses that 'disprove' the ball crossed the line are equally flawed. In January 2017, Sky TV, using the latest technology, was able to 'prove categorically' that the ball had crossed the line.

But none of this was necessary. There were moving pictures available in 1966 showing that the ball had crossed the line. But not on TV. Film cameras were at Wembley on the day for the newsreels that, despite the rise of TV, were still shown in cinemas, 48 hours after the game. British Pathé News and British Movietone News both had 10-minute features on the final, in colour. The angle on British Pathé is not clear, nor is the first piece of footage on Movietone. But Movietone used footage from a second camera, level with the goal line, which clearly shows that the ball was over. But the TV pictures have been repeated again and again, while the cinema newsreels are forgotten. England, the better team throughout the 90 minutes and extra time, thoroughly deserved to win the match, 3-2. England's fourth goal should have been disallowed, for as Kenneth Wolstenholme said, 'some people are on the pitch'.

2

PREMIER LEAGUE PLAYERS ARE *NOT* OVERPAID

Even football fans think footballers are overpaid these days. This is not new. Since the end of the maximum wage for footballers in England in 1961, after top players' wages started to climb way above the average earnings for workers, fans started to say this. The maximum wage had been £20 a week for footballers in 1961. There was an outcry when Johnny Haynes of Fulham became the first £100 a week footballer in England in that year. With Premier League players now earning on average more than £50,000 per week, and some earning £300,000 a week, surely no one, except the players themselves, can disagree that they earn too much?

Let's keep this in perspective. In England, only players in the Premier League are earning such sums. In the Championship, League One and League Two, the average wages are £350,000, £75,000 and £45,000 a year respectively. Only a tiny percentage of those who aim to be professional footballers actually make it – there are only 4,000 professional footballers in England, and most are not in the Premier League.

The big wages in the Premier League are also a comparatively recent phenomenon. In the early years of the Premier League, until the late 1990s, wages grew relatively slowly, but they have grown exponentially since, as the television rights deals of the Premier League have grown substantially. Take, for example, Neil Webb, who joined Manchester United from Nottingham Forest in 1989 for a transfer fee of £1.5 million, and returned to Forest for £800,000 in 1992. Webb won the League Cup with Forest in 1989, and with United the FA Cup in 1990, the European Cup Winners' Cup in 1991 and the League Cup in 1992. On his return to Forest, he played in the Premier League and was a Forest player until 1996. Yet he became a postman when his career ended, to earn a living.

Even if most professional players don't earn a great deal, why shouldn't the very top players get high wages? They are the best at what they do. They entertain millions, indeed billions of people. The clubs choose to pay their wages. One argument is that football is too frivolous an activity for such high pay. But we don't say there should be a salary cap on Hollywood film stars or pop stars, or celebrities famous simply for being famous. Nor on other very highly paid sports stars, across a range of sports. As soon as football went professional, in 1885, it became part of capitalism. So why should it be any different to any other capitalist industry? The players aim to get the highest wages they can. If you were them, you would too. Even when highly paid players give substantial sums to charity, to projects they are passionate about, they don't seem to be accorded the same respect as other wealthy people who do this. And other players get criticised for not giving some of their wages away. A footballer has a career that may last 15 years, at a push 20, which could be much less due to injury, and only a very small number of players earn top wages at Premier League clubs for more than a few years.

The Premier League brings thousands of fans to the UK each year as tourists – it significantly boosts our economy. In total, the Premier League earns over £4 billion a year for the UK economy and the clubs pay more than £1.6 billion a year in tax. The big wages are needed to attract and retain the best talent from around the world, which in turn makes the Premier League the most watched league around the world, England's 'Hollywood'. Whatever you think, millions of people are prepared to pay to watch the players, and so they can command these wages. Yes, Premier League players make lots of money, but so do many other people in capitalist societies. Why should we single out footballers for such criticism?

If anything, Premier League players don't receive a large enough share. The Premier League is probably the most successful league financially in the world. Yet players don't make that much money, particularly when compared with American sports. In 2016–17, Premier League players received in wages 55 per cent of the total turnover of the clubs. In contrast, the National Football League (NFL) of gridiron football in the USA guarantees players receive roughly 60 per cent of the league's revenue. In the National Basketball Association (NBA) and Major League Baseball (MLB) in the USA, that number, though not guaranteed, is probably higher. A top Premier League player making £150,000 per week sounds excessive, but there are mediocre MLB pitchers who make more than that, in a league with nothing like the money of the Premier League. Average wages are higher in both the NBA and the MLB than the Premier League. Aaron Rodgers, quarterback at the Green Bay Packers, signed the richest contract in NFL history just before the start of the 2018–19 season, worth at least £103 million over four years. The highest paid player in the Premier League at present is Alexis Sánchez, at £315,000 per week – but over four years this will be a mere £65 million.

So what's behind this view that footballers are overpaid? It is simply prejudice against the kinds of people who become Premier League players, who tend to be working class and not well educated. For some, they are just not the 'right kind of people' to be earning such money. Which is prejudice, pure and simple. Take the criticism Raheem Sterling has faced in the English media. He has been accused of being 'greedy' and having 'lavish' spending habits, including when he bought his mother a house in 2016, and he has also been mocked for flying on a low-cost airline and shopping in low-cost stores. It's none of our business what he spends his money on or how he spends it, or which tattoos he chooses to have. Arsenal and England legend Ian Wright has quite rightly called some of the media criticism of Sterling racist. Where would much of the media be without the Premier League to report and speculate on?

3

RUGBY COULD HAVE BEEN THE GLOBAL FOOTBALL GAME, RATHER THAN SOCCER

Some have argued that soccer has come to dominate the world because it is a simpler game to play than other football games, needs less equipment, or is more attractive to play and watch, but there is no evidence for any of this. Fans of each different type of football around the world think *their* game is the best to play and watch. Different football games dominate in different countries, and regions within countries. Gridiron in the USA. Rugby union in New Zealand. Australian football and rugby league in Australia. Gaelic football in Ireland. Soccer, rugby union and rugby league in different parts of England. So what explains this?

It's all about which game got there first, and became established. Take the city of Hull in England. It's a rugby (in fact rugby league) city. A rugby club was founded in the city in 1865 – Hull Football Club, or Hull FC. A second major rugby club, now Hull Kingston Rovers, was founded in 1882. These two teams, as rugby league teams, still dominate sport in the city, and in their time have been highly successful, winning 17 major trophies between them. Hull's soccer team, Hull City, was not founded until 1904. Its full name is significant – Hull City Association Football Club. Rugby union, and then from 1895 rugby league, was firmly established in the city before a soccer club was founded. Hull City has spent almost all its history in the lower divisions, apart from five seasons in the Premier League since 2008, with a highest finishing position of 16th. The club has won no major trophies. Rugby came first, and rugby still dominates.

What is true for a city can also be true for regions or indeed countries. Australian football developed in the state of Victoria in Australia from 1859 and it's still the dominant football game in the state, despite attempts to create interest in rugby league and soccer. Rugby started in the state of New South Wales in 1864 and, as rugby league, is still by far the leading football game in New South Wales and Queensland.

So soccer has become the dominant football game in most (but not all) countries in the world, simply because it was the first football game to be introduced. So how did this happen? The key is which football game came to dominate in England in the late 19th century. There was no inevitability about this. It could have been rugby rather than soccer. Rugby could then have been the football game that the British introduced around the world. Rugby could have been the global game.

So how did soccer come to dominate in England? It didn't have a great start. The Football Association (FA) was set up in London in 1863 to provide a set of rules so that the football clubs that already existed could play each other – to that point, each had its own rules. Many clubs did not agree with the FA's laws and instead formed the Rugby Football Union in 1871. Over the next two decades, it was rugby, rather than soccer, that become popular across much of England – and Wales. Which sport took off where depended on which game was introduced first.

In the 1870s, rugby and soccer began to attract paying spectators in significant numbers and both games started paying players. Many in the FA were against professionalism, but when the clubs in the north of England threatened to break away from the FA if professionalism was banned, in 1885 the FA formally accepted it. This was a close decision – soccer could have split in two at this point. Three years later, the leading soccer clubs founded the Football League, the world's first of its kind, which rapidly became enormously successful. Rugby, equally popular, if not even more popular at this time in many towns and cities, decided not to allow professionalism. Soccer chose professionalism and a league. Rugby chose amateurism and no league. This is the moment when it was effectively decided that soccer, rather than rugby, would become the world's leading football game.

As Professor Tony Collins, the world's leading historian on rugby, has shown, by these two decisions rugby lost its early advantage. The Rugby Football Union's strict insistence on amateurism led to huge conflict in the game. Players were banned and clubs were suspended. Clubs in the north, where rugby still rivalled soccer in popularity, wanted to pay their working-class players, at least to cover their loss of earnings from their jobs when they took time off to play. The Rugby Football Union rejected this, so in 1895 the major clubs in the north broke away to form their own organisation, the Northern Rugby Football Union. This became the Rugby Football League in 1922, and over time the sport became simply known as 'rugby league' football. In 1885, soccer had nearly split into two organisations over professionalism. Instead, ten years later, rugby split over the same issue. The die was cast. While rugby union and rugby league would be spread by the British to many parts of the world, it was Association football that would dominate in England and Scotland, and become the UK's number one 'football' export. But it could quite easily have been rugby…

4

ENGLISH FANS DO *NOT* CARE ABOUT THE ENGLAND TEAM, AND THEY NEVER HAVE DONE

International football is not very important to the English – fan loyalty is largely club focused, and always has been. Fans only care about the national team briefly, for a week or two, biannually, during the World Cup and the Euros, until England are knocked out. Once England are out, we enjoy the rest of the tournament, get behind another team, but the day the tournament ends, if not before, it's back to transfer speculation: 'Who looks good in the Peru team that my club could sign over the summer?'

If asked to choose between England winning the World Cup and their own team winning anything (even promotion), most English football fans would choose the latter. Some might argue this is only true for the fans of the big clubs, and point to the fact that over the last 20 years or so, the St George flags put up by fans at England games tend not to be marked Manchester United, Liverpool or Chelsea but lower division clubs like Notts County, Torquay and Port Vale. But this in itself is very telling – even at an England game, the fans will have an England flag with the name of their club proudly emblazoned on it in large letters. For example, when England played Panama at the 2018 World Cup, behind one goal was placed a huge flag with 'Notts County 1862' on it in large letters. Notts County fans are very proud of the fact that it is the world's oldest football league club! A survey found that 63 per cent of fans said their club was their number one priority, 23 per cent said their loyalties to club and country are split equally between the two, and only 14 per cent claim to put country first.

The first 100,000 crowd for a football match in England was the FA Cup Final in 1901. The first 100,000 crowd for an England international was not until 1951 (against Austria). Once the FA Cup Final moved to Wembley Stadium in 1923, crowds were over 90,000 every year, and 100,000 each year after 1950. In contrast, even England versus Scotland, the oldest football rivalry, only attracted a crowd of 37,000 at Wembley in 1924. Even into the 1950s, most England home games were not held at Wembley but at other stadiums around the country and in London, because the crowds would not be large enough to fill Wembley.

When Hungary came to play England in 1953, the Hungarians were regarded as the best team in the world. The match was billed as the 'game of the century', a big crowd was anticipated, and so it was decided to hold it at Wembley. This was only the second 100,000 crowd at Wembley for an international, but unfortunately England were humiliated by Hungary 6-3, and then lost 7-1 in Budapest in 1954. This generated a debate about what was wrong with the England team, although nothing changed significantly until Alf Ramsey was appointed as England manager in 1962.

Even with the World Cup being held in England in 1966, there was little build-up. When England played Yugoslavia at Wembley on 4 May 1966, just two months before the World Cup began, the crowd was only 55,000. At the FA Cup Final on 14 May, ten days later, the crowd was 100,000. Even during the World Cup itself, Wembley was far from full for England's matches. For the group games against Uruguay, Mexico and France, the crowds were 87,148, 92,750 and 98,270 respectively. England's quarter-final against Argentina attracted 90,584 and the semi-final against Portugal 94,493. Even the World Cup Final itself against West Germany did not attract 100,000 – the attendance was 96,924! Throughout the tournament, tickets were fairly easy to come by, even for England games. Many fans with tickets didn't even go to some England matches, including the final. I have met a man who as a boy of 12 in 1966 had a ticket for the final but his mum wouldn't let him go! A family who had tickets for all the England games, including the final, stopped going to Wembley because the view wasn't very good and it was easier and better to watch at home on TV – in black and white! When world champions England played Wales at Wembley in November 1966, the crowd was only 75,000.

The rise of the Premier League has intensified club loyalties above the England team. English football fans care passionately about their club, not their country. England exceeded all expectations in the 2018 World Cup by finishing fourth. Yet at their first game at Wembley after the World Cup, against Spain, there were almost 10,000 empty seats…

5

FIFA DOES *NOT* MAKE THE RULES, AND NEVER HAS

If you ever complain about FIFA messing around with the rules of the game, then you need to know: FIFA does not make the rules. First, this is because football has laws, not rules. And second, because the laws are controlled and amended by a little-known body called the International Football Association Board (IFAB). And we Brits control it, so we should blame ourselves!

Although by the early 1880s the rules of football had been more or less standardised, the UK's four football associations – England, Scotland, Wales and Ireland – still used slightly different regulations. This was somewhat problematic for internationals, so when the national sides met, the home team's rulebook was used. This worked, but wasn't exactly ideal, so the four associations met in Manchester in 1882 to agree a common set of laws for the occasions when they played each other. Out of this meeting came a proposal to set up a permanent board, responsible for regulating the game, and the British Home Championship, between England,

Scotland, Ireland and Wales. This was the world's oldest international competition and it first took place in 1884. In 1886, the IFAB met for the first time in London and the four nations were given equal voting rights over the laws.

Football spread across Europe, and in 1904 FIFA (Fédération Internationale de Football Association) was formed in Paris. FIFA recognised the need for a uniform set of rules for the game, but decided to accept the laws already established by the IFAB. The Football Association (the English FA) joined FIFA in 1905, but the FAs of Scotland and Wales did not join FIFA until 1910, and that of Ireland in 1911. In 1913 FIFA representatives were allowed to join the IFAB. Initially, they only had two votes, the same number as each of the UK associations, and decisions required a four-fifths majority to pass, meaning that the UK associations could still change the laws against FIFA's wishes if they all voted together. With the partition of Ireland in 1921, the Irish Football Association became the organising body for football in Northern Ireland. A new body was established for football in the Republic of Ireland, the Football Association of Ireland, but this was not allowed to join the IFAB.

In 1958 FIFA joined the IFAB as a full member, and was given the same voting power as the original four associations put together, so each UK association has one vote and FIFA has four. Any change to the laws must be approved by three-quarters of the vote – that is, six votes. Thus FIFA's approval is necessary for any IFAB decision, but FIFA alone cannot change the laws – they need to be agreed by at least two of the UK members. As of 2016, all members must be present for a binding vote to proceed.

So, the four British FAs have 50 per cent control of the laws of the game, and effectively a veto over any changes. As the game has now spread to over 200 countries, the fairness of this has been questioned several times. The IFAB's introductory page on its website states: 'The IFAB is comprised of the four British football associations (England, Scotland, Wales and Northern Ireland) with one vote each, and FIFA, covering the remaining 207 national associations, with four votes.' FIFA has consistently defended the status quo, using history as the reason – that the British invented the game and established IFAB as the keeper of the rules, which FIFA then joined. So next time you get annoyed by a law change, don't blame FIFA!

6

ENGLAND DID *NOT* WIN THE WORLD CUP FAIRLY IN 1966

So the ball was over the line and England won the final of the World Cup in 1966 fair and square. But England did not win the *tournament* fairly. Everything was stacked in England's favour, even before the finals began.

When qualification started, FIFA had 120 member countries, but only 74 of these initially entered. Then a further 21 nations withdrew because the qualification system was so biased against the African and Asian countries. The global view of England as competent hosts was severely dented when the Jules Rimet Trophy – the World Cup – was stolen in March 1966 from a stamp exhibition in London, luckily to be found under a hedge in a suburban street by a dog called Pickles seven days later.

England qualified for the finals as hosts. In the group matches, they played poorly in a goalless draw against Uruguay, were better in beating Mexico, but were very lucky against France. The first England goal was clearly offside and the second was scored while a French player lay injured after a bad, unpunished foul.

In the quarter-final against Argentina, England began with a number of bad fouls on the opposition – the very high foul count at the end of the game was 33 fouls committed by England and 19 by Argentina. And yet Alf Ramsey called the Argentinians 'animals' after the match and refused to let his players swap shirts. An Argentinian player at half time told a journalist: 'They are kicking the shit out of us.' After 35 minutes, Argentina's captain, Antonio Rattín, became the first player to be sent off in a senior international football match at Wembley, for a second bookable offence, which the referee described afterwards as 'violence of the tongue', despite him speaking no Spanish. Rattín's intention appeared to have been to speak with the West German referee, to complain that he was consistently ruling in favour of the England team. Rattín made a visible signal showing his captain's armband and his desire to call for a translator. No wonder the game is known as 'el robo del siglo' (the robbery of the century) in Argentina. The Argentinian team were welcomed as heroes on their return home and the Argentinian FA talked openly about leaving FIFA altogether, as England in their view had been so favoured, at a time when the president of FIFA was an Englishman, Sir Stanley Rous.

They were not the only ones unimpressed with the referee. In *The Sunday Times*, the leading football journalist Brian Glanville described him as 'a small man, strutting portentously about the field … as he put name after Argentinian name into his notebook. One was reminded of a schoolboy collecting railway engine numbers.' Many neutrals also took the same view. An Italian newspaper had the headline 'Scandal in London – too much favouritism for the England team', and called Rattín's dismissal 'a colossal injustice which offended against the very essence of sport'. Eusébio, whose Portugal team would play England next in the semi-final, said 'The referee always seemed to see only the worst faults of the Argentina players. He could not see the faults of the England players.'

After the final, England's World Cup win was not respected around the globe, only in part because of the grainy TV pictures of their controversial third goal in the final. Strong anti-English feeling was demonstrated all over South America. The British Embassy in

Uruguay reported that the result had been 'to raise doubts in the minds of normally friendly people as to whether the traditional British "fair play" really exists now'. The Foreign Office reported that 'Sportswriters in the Italian press were universally critical of the organisation of the World Cup, and in particular of the choice and performance of the referees.' In Bolivia, the country's biggest-selling newspaper commented that England had 'sold its hard-earned reputation for chivalry, for fair play and for correctness, for a football trophy. Today there are thousands of people who have always admired England who no longer admire England. England may now be the world champions but it is no longer the country of culture, of education, of gentlemen.'

Let's give the final word to Edson Arantes do Nascimento, who is better known as Pelé. Pelé had been kicked out of the tournament through a lack of protection by the referees: 'The games had been a revelation to me in their unsportsmanlike conduct and weak refereeing. England won the games that year but in my opinion she did not have the best team ... football stopped being an art, stopped drawing the crowds by its skills, instead it became an actual war.' England may have won the World Cup, but the tournament was poor, ill received around the world, and the widespread view that England had won unfairly severely damaged the country's standing. Jules Rimet still gleaming?

7

BRITISH PLAYERS *CAN* AND *HAVE* SUCCEEDED ABROAD

There is a long-standing perception that English, indeed British, players cannot succeed abroad. They are somehow too insular, get homesick, can't or won't learn the language, are just too British. Whereas those from overseas (as long as they can adapt to the cold and wet climate, and the food!) can succeed in England. But this simply isn't true. British players – and coaches and managers – have been going abroad and succeeding right from the beginning of the game. After all, the British played a key role – if not the only role – in spreading the game to over 200 countries.

In 1891, Herbert Kilpin, an English footballer and Nottingham native with experience in the lace trade, moved to Turin in Italy, to work for a textile merchant called Edoardo Bosio. That year, Bosio founded Italy's first football club, Internazionale Torino. Kilpin was enlisted to play for the team, which probably made him the first Englishman to play football abroad, and participated in the first two seasons of the Italian Football

Championship. In 1898, Kilpin left Turin and went to Milan where he met up with another Englishman, Mancunian Samuel Davies, who also had textile industry connections. The following year the two men were among the founder members of the Milan Football and Cricket Club, as AC Milan was originally called. Yet another Englishman, Alfred Edwards, was elected as the club's first president, and Kilpin, their most experienced footballer, became player-manager. The newly founded team was an instant success, winning the national title in 1901 (which was only their second season), and in 1906 and 1907, all under Kilpin's leadership. Kilpin stayed at the club for nine seasons, making a total of 23 appearances and scoring seven goals. There are countless other examples of such success throughout the first half of the 20th century for British players and also coaches and managers, and yet they are largely unknown and not recognised in the UK.

John Charles is the one player up to the 1960s who is more widely known to have succeeded abroad. In August 1957 he moved from Leeds United to Italian club Juventus for what was then a record British transfer fee of £65,000. During his first season in Italy he scored

28 goals, which made him Serie A's top scorer; Juventus won the league and Charles himself was voted player of the season. In 1959 he was third in the European Footballer of the Year competition. He stayed at Turin for five seasons, winning the league three times and the Italian Cup twice, and scoring 108 goals in 155 matches. In 1997, when Juventus was celebrating its centenary, fans demonstrated their esteem for him by voting Charles the club's best-ever foreign player.

Denis Law, by comparison, is often cited as a player who didn't make it abroad. Law moved from Manchester City to Torino in Italy in 1961 for a fee of £110,000 – again, at the time a record transfer fee for a British player. While he was not happy, he was a success – he was voted number one foreign player in Italy – but he didn't like the heavily defensive play or the aggressive marking. In 1962 he joined Manchester United for another new British record fee of £115,000 – and the rest is history.

By the late 1970s, 1980s and early 1990s, many British players were lured abroad – most often by higher wages. And almost all of them succeeded. For example: Kevin Keegan (twice European Footballer of the Year at Hamburg), Ian Rush, Paul Gascoigne, Liam Brady, Tony

Woodcock, Chris Waddle, Glenn Hoddle, Gary Lineker, David Platt, Steve McManaman and Graeme Souness. Players not quite at this level also tried their luck and in many cases succeeded. Michael Robinson left Liverpool for Osasuna in Spain in 1987 and, after retiring as a player in 1989, became a highly successful Spanish television pundit. Such is his love of the country that he stayed and became a Spanish citizen. Robinson has also worked as a voice-over artist on TV ads and films. He even voiced the Ugly Stepsister role for the Spanish versions of the *Shrek* movies! When John Aldridge moved from Liverpool to Real Sociedad in 1989, he was the first non-Basque player to sign for the club since the late 1960s, after the club finally dropped its ban on foreign imports. Aldridge was highly successful, scoring 40 goals in 75 appearances. Dalian Atkinson joined him there for a season, scoring 12 goals in 29 games, and they were the most potent pair of strikers in La Liga that season. British managers, including Bobby Robson, Terry Venables and John Toshack, have also been highly successful abroad.

So why do we have this view that the British do not succeed abroad? Part of it is that before international football TV saturation, we tended not to see them. Partly, we were annoyed that they had left us. And partly, for most football fans the idea that you could successfully live and work abroad at this time was unthinkable. As our own horizons have widened in the last two decades, British footballers playing and succeeding abroad has come to seem natural and obvious, and to some extent increasingly essential. The influx of foreign players into Britain means that British players struggle to get into high-level teams here – and so have to look abroad.

This is exemplified by the recent success of Jadon Sancho at Borussia Dortmund. Let's hope for many more…

8

SOCCER, AND *NOT* AMERICAN FOOTBALL, COULD HAVE BEEN THE MAIN WINTER SPORT IN THE USA

While rugby could have been the world's number one sport, so Association football rather than American football could have been the winter sport of the USA. Contrary to popular myth, professional soccer in America did not begin with the arrival of Pelé in 1975. In fact, America's first attempt at professional soccer took place in 1894, with the formation of the American League of Professional Football (ALPF). Pre-dating the formation of professional gridiron football and basketball leagues by many years, the ALPF was a great opportunity for soccer to become one of the key sports in the USA – indeed, the main winter sport. But the opportunity was lost.

On paper, the time seemed ideal for a professional soccer league. Baseball had thrived as a professional sport for over 20 years. Moreover, England's Football League, started in 1888 and modelled on the American baseball league, was already a success. In 1894 soccer was already well established in the USA as an amateur sport. The American Football Association (AFA) had successfully staged the American Cup tournament for over a decade, and there was a developing fan base for soccer. The game had also grown from its original base in the north-eastern United States, and had ceased to be the exclusive preserve of immigrants.

In August 1894, six owners of National League baseball clubs met in New York to announce the formation of the American League of Professional Football Clubs (ALPF), namely Philadelphia, Baltimore, Boston, Brooklyn, New York and Washington. Their intention was to draw the baseball crowds to soccer and make money in baseball's winter off-season, and so the soccer clubs were all named after their respective baseball teams. The ALPF was visionary, as the rules were to be 'the same as those in use in England, with the exception of a few minor changes', including substitutions.

The amateur AFA tried to stop it, banning any of its players from joining the new league, but the baseball club owners had the money to draw the best players and the top-quality stadiums to put them in. The players attracted were mainly the best English and Irish players from local leagues. Baltimore even went as far as to sign four players from Manchester City and one from Sheffield United!

The season began and all seemed very promising. So why didn't it work? The baseball owners behind the league suddenly had a more pressing concern. As the soccer season began, rumours of a second professional baseball league caused them to become very cautious financially, fearing a bidding war for players with this potential second league. Suddenly, the luxury of operating soccer clubs in the hope of filling baseball stadiums during the off-season was something no one could afford. The US government also announced its intention to investigate the Baltimore Orioles' importation of British professional soccer players. The league owners decided that the time had come to pull the plug on the venture. So a mere six games into the season, the ALPF stopped. The cancellation of the 1894 season was not originally intended to be the death of the league. Instead, the owners hoped to reorganise play for the spring of 1895 and, indeed, several owners seem to have become true converts to the game by the end of the year. However, the continued government investigation meant that this did not happen, and so the moment was lost.

If the ALPF had been successful, sport in America would be very different today. Ironically, the league's hundredth anniversary could have been celebrated during the 1994 FIFA World Cup held in the United States. Instead, it was a golden opportunity wasted.

9

MOST FANS ARE *NOT* LOYAL TO ONE CLUB – THEY PLAY THE FIELD

The idea that most fans are loyal throughout their life to just one club is a complete myth. In the myth, the young fan (always a boy), aged five or six (or even younger), is taken to his first game by his father, and immediately swears total and unquestioning allegiance to his father's team for the rest of his life. And it was his grandfather's team, and *his* father's before that, back to the foundation of the club. But of course, this is completely untrue. Those fans who claim to be undying in their support are often lying, and have dabbled with other teams – not least when they are youngsters in school, when, due to peer pressure, almost every child has to support one of the big clubs.

There are a very small number of fans who genuinely follow the likes of Torquay United, home and away, every game. But these are figures of fun in the tabloid media, because the story is usually how their wife or partner gave them the ultimatum of 'it's your football team or me', and they chose the football team. So they now only have access to their children at weekends – but they can't see them because they are following their team on an 18-hour away trip to Carlisle United.

Studies have shown that the vast majority of football fans are not like this. Almost no season ticket holders go to every game in a season at home. This is why there are sometimes empty seats, even at Manchester United. Often the season ticket seat is occupied not by the season ticket holder, but by a friend or relative. Some clubs have calculated their season ticket price on the basis that even the keen fans will only be able to go to 15 or so games in a season. People have other things in their lives, like family and friends, weddings and holidays. There is generally around 10 per cent turnover in season ticket holders even at big clubs at the end of each season, as people's lives change – for example, they move away for work, or they can no longer afford a season ticket. If all fans were die-hards, how do we explain the massive fall in gates when a team is doing badly? Most fans quite rightly are not prepared to pay to watch lousy football followed by relegation. They will come back when the team is doing well. This is not glory-hunting, this is common sense.

Most fans of lower league clubs also pick a Premier League team to follow, even though this is not their number one loyalty. I support Tranmere Rovers, currently in the third tier of English football, and Everton are my Premier League team. But on the rare occasions when Tranmere play Everton, I am 100 per cent supporting Tranmere, and was never happier than on 27 January 2001 when Tranmere beat Everton 3-0 in the fourth round of the FA Cup at Goodison Park! But many fans have more than one team that they support, even if they support the others less strongly. English fans traditionally picked a Scottish team they liked the name of when they were a child. Think of those poetic Scottish football club names like Partick Thistle, Heart of Midlothian or Queen of the South. We then follow their results, without ever going to a game. My Scottish team, since 1968, has been Stenhousemuir. I have never been to a game and I do not know where Stenhousemuir is. This doesn't matter, I still follow their results. Now with global football on our TV screens and online 24 hours a day, 365 days a year, we can support any team, anywhere in the world. In the World Cup, most English fans have another national team they support, because they like the way they play (it's usually better than England!), or they have one of their club's players, or just to have someone to follow after England get knocked out.

Football support also has a life cycle. You might be very keen aged 9 to 12 but move on to other things in your teenage years. If you find a partner, and particularly if you then have children, you may stop going to football, at least until the children are older. But you may never go back to it, especially if they turn out not to be interested. Mine weren't! There is so much choice in life now in terms of leisure time that devoting it to football seems very old-fashioned and limiting.

Fans have also historically often gone to watch more than one team, though with high ticket prices, especially in England, this has declined. Teams like Tranmere Rovers and Stockport County used to play their home games on Friday nights, as hundreds if not thousands of Liverpool and Everton fans came to Tranmere and Manchester City and Manchester United fans went to Stockport, as well as going to see their own team on the Saturday. At least a thousand English fans travel to watch Borussia Dortmund every home game, because of the atmosphere, and many fans take short breaks to go and watch teams across Europe. Many fans profess undying love and support for their team, but a large number have become rather fickle. Just as we can love more than one person, we can love more than one football team – it's not exclusive, though there probably always has to be the 'special one'. And as in romantic love, in football you can fall out of love altogether, and find a new love.

Nick Hornby's *Fever Pitch* is held up as the book that best expresses this undying loyalty to one club – in his case, Arsenal. Except that in *Fever Pitch* there is a long period in his life when Hornby stopped going to watch Arsenal, being more interested in girls, music, drinking and literature (the first three at least being typical late teenage behaviour), and for a time watching Cambridge United (less so). *Fever Pitch* is not about undying love for one team, it's about how our interests and obsessions change as we change, and how sometimes we come back to them. Hornby has gone back to football in the same way that many middle-aged men go back to their boyhood obsession with collecting the likes of stamps – or football cards…

10

BLACK PLAYERS ARE *NOT* NEW IN ENGLISH FOOTBALL

Ask the average English fan and they will probably think black players came into the game in the 1980s. But it was in fact the 1880s. And the first was Scottish. Before professional football had begun (or at least been legitimised), Andrew Watson was a leading amateur player and the world's first black person to compete at international level.

Watson was born in 1856 in British Guiana (now Guyana); his father was a wealthy Scottish sugar plantation owner and his mother was Guianese. He later came to Britain, where he played football both at school and at the University of Glasgow. In 1880 he signed for Queen's Park, which was then Britain's largest, albeit still amateur, team. He achieved several Scottish Cups with the club, making him the first black player to win major honours.

The following year he won the first of his three international caps for Scotland, in a match against England in which he was also captain. Scotland won 6-1.

His entry in the 1880–81 *Scottish Football Association Annual* praised Watson's great speed, splendid tackling and powerful kick, concluding that he was 'well worthy of a place in any representative team'. In 1926, a leading sports journalist selected him as the left-back in his 'all-time' Scotland team.

Watson moved to London in the summer of 1882, which ended his international career as the Scottish Football Association only selected players who were based in Scotland, but the year after that he became the first black player to play in the English FA Cup and the first non-English player to be invited to join a leading English amateur club, Corinthian.

In 1887 Watson moved to Bootle on Merseyside. Professionalism was now permitted by the English FA and the club was known to offer signing fees and wages to players, so Watson could have been a professional. If he was paid, his professional status would have pre-dated the career of Arthur Wharton, who is generally considered to be the world's first black footballer to play professionally.

Arthur Wharton was born in Jamestown, Gold Coast, in what is now Accra in Ghana. His father was from Grenada in the West Indies and his mother was of Ghanaian royalty. In 1882, when he was 19, Wharton came to England with the aim of training as a Methodist missionary, but he quickly dropped his religious studies to become a full-time sportsman. An excellent all-rounder, who enjoyed cricket and cycling, at the 1886 Amateur Athletic Association of England Championship he equalled the world record of 10 seconds for the 100-yard sprint. He began playing amateur football in goal for Darlington, but then joined Preston North End, also as an amateur, and was with the team when it reached the 1886–87 FA Cup semi-finals. He left Preston in 1888 to focus on athletics, so was not part of the 'Invincibles' team that won the world's first football league and first 'double', but he later returned to football and played as a professional at Rotherham Town and other clubs.

So black players have been part of the game in England – and Scotland – from the very beginning. And players coming from South America and Africa to play in the UK is not new either – Andrew Watson and Arthur Wharton did this in the 1880s!

11

THE ENGLISH *DIDN'T* SPREAD FOOTBALL TO BRAZIL – IT WAS THE *GERMANS*

Anyone with knowledge of football history around the world knows the game began in England. In each country, they tell you very proudly that the English brought the game to their country, over a century ago. At the National Football Museum for England in Manchester, visitors have come from over 150 countries, and many write in the visitors' comments book simply: 'Thank you for the beautiful game.' Everyone wants to believe the English brought them the game; it gives them authenticity, their football came from the 'DNA' of the game, from the 'mother' nation of football. The only problem is that it is very often a myth – it wasn't the English at all, but other nations that brought the game to their country, whether other Europeans or in South America, for example, other South Americans.

In Brazil, they *know* the English brought them the game. They even know the name of the Englishman who brought it, Charles Miller. There is a street named after him in São Paulo, and a statue. The only problem is it's not true.

For a start, Charles Miller wasn't English. Charles Miller was Brazilian. He was born in São Paulo in 1874. His parents weren't English either. His father was a Scottish railway engineer and his mother was a Brazilian of English descent. In 1884, at the age of nine, Charles was sent to be educated at a private school in Southampton, England. There he learned to be a proper English gentleman, and this of course included sport. The sports he learned were cricket, rugby and football, but the school's headmaster during Miller's time there increasingly favoured football over rugby. Had Miller gone to a different private school, it could quite easily have been – and was indeed much more likely – that he would have played just rugby and cricket. So it's only by chance that Miller learned Association football at all, and didn't instead take a rugby ball back with him to Brazil. So perhaps Brazil might have become a great rugby nation!

So did this Brazilian of partial Scottish descent then bring soccer to Brazil? When he returned to Brazil in

1894, Miller took two footballs and a set of Hampshire Football Association rules in his suitcase. There is evidence that other Brits had played football in Brazil prior to Miller, but not in such an organised way. With several British immigrants, Miller set up the football team of the São Paulo Athletic Club (SPAC). He also played cricket, which had been prevalent in the British community in São Paulo since the 1870s. In 1902, Miller and others set up the first São Paulo state tournament, the Liga Paulista, the first football league in Brazil. SPAC won the first three championships in 1902, 1903 and 1904, Miller himself being the leading goal scorer in 1902. But they did not want to share football with the 'native' Brazilians. Miller and his associates only wished to play against middle-class Europeans, with the 'Anglo-Saxons', not the 'natives'. When Brazilians, including the working-class and ethnic minorities, took up the sport, Miller and his colleagues were not willing to play them. In 1912 SPAC retired from official football competitions, although the sport continued to be played at the club, but only for recreation. To maintain the separate position of the higher-class Europeans, rugby became the main sport of the club, and they also took up tennis. They were not interested in spreading football to the Brazilians. Indeed, once it had spread by other means, they gave it up!

The Germans have at least as good, if not an even better claim to have brought and spread football in Brazil. Hans Nobiling arrived in São Paulo from Germany in 1897 and set up a team. A team was also established by locals at Mackenzie College. When in 1899 the college approached Charles Miller's São Paulo Athletic Club, made up entirely of British players, for a match, SPAC refused, preferring to play among themselves. The college then approached Nobiling's team and they agreed to play. It was a 0-0 draw, but almost certainly the first inter-club fixture in the history of Brazilian football. Nobiling's team, now named SC Germânia to show its German roots, also played in the first Brazilian league in 1902. There is both a street and a cultural centre named after Nobiling in São Paulo. Germans (and later Italians) settled in very much greater numbers in Brazil than the British and so played a much greater role in spreading the game around the country. The first great Brazilian player was Arthur Friedenreich, who was born in 1892 in São Paulo to Oscar Friedenreich, a man of German descent but born in

Brazil, and Mathilde, an African Brazilian washerwoman and the daughter of freed slaves. Friedenreich was also the first professional football player of Afro-Brazilian origin. He started his career playing for Nobiling's SC Germânia...

12

THERE'S *NO* SUCH PROBLEM AS SCORING TOO EARLY

No one is more superstitious than football fans – except perhaps football players! One of the fans' biggest superstitions is that a team can damage its chances by scoring too early. The other team has time to come back and win the game, and therefore it's better to score the opening goal later in the game. Instead of building on the early advantage, scoring early gives the initiative to the trailing side. But this simply isn't true. With football being such a low-scoring game, especially when compared with many other sports, it's much better to score first. The superstition perhaps derives from another piece of psychology – fans don't want their team to score in the first few minutes as there has been no build-up, not enough expectation, it's just too soon to enjoy the goal. There has been no equivalent of foreplay!

In total, there have been 2,802 opening goals during the first 15 minutes of Premier League games since 1992, more than during any other interval. Interestingly, that number reduces in 15-minute increments, with

2,173 opening goals scored between 16 and 30 minutes, 1,710 between 31 and 45 minutes, 1,002 from 46 to 60 minutes, 690 during 61 to 75 minutes, and 516 during 76 to 90 minutes. But are teams that score the opening goal early less likely to win than a side that scores it later? The answer is yes, the odds of winning improve when a team scores an opening goal later in a game. However, even an early goal still on average significantly improves the chances of victory. Over the last 25 years, teams that scored within the first 15 minutes won 63 per cent of the time. If the opening goal was struck between the 16th and 30th minutes, that win rate rises marginally to 66 per cent, reaching 70 per cent if scored during the final 15 minutes of the first half. Teams that score the first goal of the game within 15 minutes of the restart have a 73 per cent win rate, and there is a considerable rise to 78 per cent for sides that open the scoring between the 61st and 75th minutes. That rate soars to 89 per cent during the final 15 minutes, which still allows an 11 per cent chance for the trailing team to steal a point or three – so at 1-0 up, it really isn't over until the final whistle.

But all of this doesn't mean that your team should put everything into defence, stop the opposition scoring, and then score in the last 15 minutes. Score first, even in the first 15 minutes, and you win two games out of every three. And this is just winning; scoring first and drawing needs to be added to this. Draws are around another 18 per cent overall from scoring first, which means losing after scoring first is about a 20 per cent chance in the first 15 minutes, going down to less than 5 per cent in the last 15 minutes.

Scoring the first goal at home is more valuable than away. Scoring first at home means a team will go on to win 74 per cent of games compared with 64 per cent when scoring first as the away team, a difference of 10 per cent.

Football is a relatively low scoring sport, so there's no such thing as scoring too early. Even if you missed it because you were queueing for a pie and a pint!

13

CAMBRIDGE AND *NOT* SHEFFIELD IS HOME TO THE WORLD'S OLDEST FOOTBALL CLUB

Founded in 1857, Sheffield FC is officially recognised by FIFA as the oldest Association football club in the world. Sheffield FC received a FIFA Centennial Order of Merit in 2004. In 2007, the then FIFA President, Joseph 'Sepp' Blatter, went to Sheffield to mark the 150th anniversary of the club. The organisers of the Qatar 2022 FIFA World Cup have also recognised Sheffield FC as the club 'where the rules of the game were born'. The only problem with this is that it isn't true. Sheffield FC has an important role in the history of the game. But it isn't this one.

For a start, Sheffield FC couldn't have been an Association football club until 1863, because Association football hadn't been invented. Instead, Sheffield FC played games under the Sheffield Rules, drawn up in 1858 and published the following year, and in 1863 did not adopt the FA rules but continued to play its own 'Sheffield' form of football, which in some aspects was more like rugby, until 1878.

But Sheffield FC isn't the oldest Association football club still playing today, because this is Cambridge University Association Football Club, which was founded a year earlier, in 1856. Of course, the Cambridge club wasn't founded as an Association football club either, as it couldn't be yet, but it had its own Cambridge laws – and these Cambridge laws, dating from 1856 and therefore older than the Sheffield FC laws, were the major reference point and influence on the FA's laws established in 1863. There is a strong case that Association football actually effectively began in Cambridge. It's possible that the Cambridge University Football Club was founded in 1846, and certainly Cambridge laws existed by 1848, and were posted on trees around Parker's Piece, the park in the centre of Cambridge where games were played. 'The Laws of the University Foot Ball Club' survive from 1856, and are remarkably similar to the FA's first laws in 1863.

The Cambridge Laws of 1856 even had an offside rule: 'If the ball has passed a player and has come from the direction of his own goal, he may not touch it till the other side have kicked it, unless there are more than three of the other side before him. No player is allowed to loiter between the ball and the adversaries' goal.' Cambridge University has produced a commemorative postcard with a visual representation of the offside rule law, and the words: 'Dear World, You can blame us for the offside rule. Sorry.' But they don't need to apologise – the offside law is one of the great inventions of football, preventing goal-hanging and enormously improving the game.

The revised 1863 Cambridge laws, published just before the first meeting of the FA, were even more similar to what the FA then developed. Not surprising, as the first FA secretary, Ebenezer Cobb Morley, who drafted the first laws of the game, said at the time of the Cambridge laws: 'They embrace the true principles of the game, with the greatest simplicity.' Charles Alcock, the man who would go on to invent the FA Cup and international football in 1872 (oh, and Test Match cricket in 1880), said: 'The Cambridge Rules appear to be the most desirable for the Association to adopt.'

The Cambridge University Association Football Club also played a key role in establishing on-field positions, a passing game and effective teamwork. The 1883 Cambridge side was credited by Charles Alcock as being 'the first to illustrate the full possibilities of a systematic combination giving full scope to the defence as well as the attack'.

In 2008, the National Football Museum inducted Sheffield FC into its Hall of Fame as the 'world's oldest football club'. While still recognising the historical importance of the Sheffield club, in 2016 the Museum inducted Cambridge University Association Football Club as the world's oldest football club. Better late than never...

14

ARSENAL SHOULD *NOT* BE
IN THE PREMIER LEAGUE

Arsenal were promoted to the top flight of English football in an incredibly dubious way in 1919 – at the expense of arch-rivals Tottenham Hotspur – and have never been relegated since.

After the First World War began in August 1914, league football continued, the football authorities arguing that it was good for morale. After facing fierce criticism that it was unpatriotic – rugby union had stopped almost straight away – the Football League suspended competition at the end of the 1914–15 season. Even though the war hadn't ended, as initially expected, by Christmas 1914, it was still widely believed that it would soon be over. But it was not until the 1919–20 season that league football could begin again.

In March 1919, the Football League met to consider a number of proposals for a new structure. It agreed to increase both the then top division, called the First Division, and the Second Division, from 20 to 22 teams. Derby County and Preston North End, who had finished first and second in the Second Division, were promoted. On past precedent, the two other places would be given to the two clubs that would otherwise have been relegated from the First Division, namely Chelsea and Tottenham Hotspur.

Chelsea were given a place, but, very oddly, not Tottenham. The reason given for Chelsea was that the game between Manchester United and Liverpool on 2 April 1915 had been fixed in Manchester United's favour. The upshot was that Manchester United avoided relegation by one point, relegating Chelsea. But why weren't Tottenham given the other place? No good reason was given. One might think, therefore, that instead the team that had finished third in the second division, Barnsley, would be promoted, if Spurs were to be relegated. Yet, bizarrely, the Football League decided to have a ballot, and the candidates were: 20th-placed Tottenham Hotspur and, from the Second Division, Barnsley (3rd), Wolves (4th), Birmingham (5th), Arsenal (6th), Hull City (7th) and Nottingham Forest (18th!). Arsenal, on the same points as Birmingham, should have finished fifth on goal average, but this was calculated incorrectly at the time. Arsenal were retrospectively awarded fifth place in 1975!

Arsenal's chairman, Sir Henry Norris, apparently argued that Arsenal should be promoted for their 'long service to league football'. The League board agreed, though Wolves in particular had a much longer history, as they were founder members in 1888. Arsenal received 18 votes, Tottenham 8, Barnsley 5, Wolves 4, with a further 6 votes shared between the other clubs. Very suspiciously, no records of the meeting can be found, and yet all other meetings of the Football League at this time were very well documented.

It appears that the announcement that there would be a vote seemed to catch all the clubs, except Arsenal, unawares. It has been alleged that Arsenal's promotion was down to backroom deals or even outright bribery by Norris, colluding with his friend John McKenna, the chairman of both Liverpool and the Football League, who had recommended Arsenal's promotion at the league's annual general meeting.

In 1927, the *Daily Mail* accused Norris of making illegal payments to Sunderland player Charlie Buchan as an inducement to encourage him to join Arsenal. Although some clubs did break the rules, the league's maximum wage policy was strictly enforced. The Football

Association investigated and discovered that Norris had also paid his personal chauffeur from his Arsenal expenses account and had kept £125 from the proceeds of the sale of the team bus. Norris sued the *Daily Mail* and the FA for libel, but in 1929 the law courts found against him and Norris subsequently received a life ban from football. He resigned as chairman of Arsenal and left the club.

One theory is that the match fixing issues of the 1914–15 season were used by Norris as a weapon in his battle to get Arsenal promoted. He demanded that Liverpool and Manchester United (some of whose players had been found guilty of match fixing) be punished by relegation or expulsion, and threatened to organise a breakaway from the league by clubs from the Midlands and the south of England if nothing was done. To placate him, it is claimed, the league offered Arsenal a place in the First Division.

Regardless of the reason, Arsenal should not have been promoted in 1919 to the First Division, which became the Premier League in 1992, and therefore should not be in the Premier League. And Tottenham should not have been relegated in 1919. No wonder they are such bitter rivals...

15

LEICESTER CITY WILL *NEVER* WIN THE PREMIER LEAGUE AGAIN

It was a massive shock when Leicester City, as rank outsiders, won the Premier League in 2016. The bookmakers had to pay out on bets placed at the start of the season at odds of 5,000–1 that Leicester would win. Some said this proved that the Premier League is exciting and competitive, and that any team can win it. But this isn't true. Leicester City will never win the Premier League again. And no team like Leicester City will ever win it again, unless there is fundamental, if not revolutionary, change to the Premier League.

Reacting to Leicester winning the Premier League, its executive chairman, Richard Scudamore, said: 'If this was a once in every 5,000-year event, then we've effectively got another 5,000 years of hope ahead of us.' But that's not how it works. Bookmakers always win in the long run. It means it is extremely unlikely to happen again; the slim chance has come, been taken and gone. The day after Leicester won, the team's manager, Claudio Ranieri, said he did not believe Leicester

City could win the Premier League title again in the foreseeable future: 'No. I think no, but of course we want to continue to build. When I came here, the project was to build a foundation and to fight for the Europa League in three to four years.' He said that Leicester's target for the next season was to finish 'in the top ten... We want a good campaign in Europe and in the cups, and we want to be sure next season that we are safe, and then to do something more.' Ranieri cautioned against excessive hope of Leicester retaining the title, arguing that the other clubs now understood Leicester's counter-attacking tactics.

And so it proved. Jamie Vardy, who had scored 24 goals when they won the league, struggled for the first half of the next season and scored only 13 all season. Ranieri was right. Too right. In February, with Leicester just one point above the relegation zone, he was sacked. Leicester eventually finished 12th, mid-table – which, based on their financial resources, was where they would have been expected to finish. In the year before they won the league, they had finished 14th. Since they won the league, they have finished 12th and 9th twice. Mid-table, where they would be expected to be.

So how on earth did they win in 2016? I don't want to take anything away from the manager, the players and the fans. They had great team spirit, good tactics, and great leadership by Ranieri. The most used starting team cost a mere £23 million. Ranieri made only 27 changes to his starting eleven all season – way down on the average of 95 for Premier League champions. He didn't have the squad size and choices of the top six, and he therefore developed an excellent counter-attacking approach, which worked particularly well in the first half of the season. Leicester were ranked 18th out of 20 for possession in the season, with just 42 per cent of possession, as opposed to, for example, Arsenal, who came second, with 59 per cent. Leicester were ranked 18th out of 20 in the number of passes, 12,586, compared with Arsenal's highest figure of 20,257. They even came lowest in the whole league in terms of passing accuracy, below even the three teams that were relegated, with just 70 per cent, compared with Arsenal's 84 per cent. But they made those passes count. It was an extraordinary achievement. Which is why it won't happen again.

Leicester also won because the top six lost it. If we look at the Premier League's top six in the 2014–15 season, the season before Leicester won, Chelsea were champions with 87 points, followed by Manchester City with 79, Arsenal 75, Manchester United 70, Tottenham Hotspur 64 and Liverpool 62. In the 2015–16 season, Leicester won with 81 points, followed by Arsenal with 71, Spurs 70, Manchester United and Manchester City 66, and Liverpool back in 8th with a mere 60 points. In the 2016–17 season Chelsea won with 93 points, followed by Spurs with 86, Manchester City 78, Liverpool 76, Arsenal 75 and Manchester United with 69.

The bookies were right. Leicester winning the Premier League was a 5,000–1 shot. They, or a team from their level, may not win it for another 5,000 years.

16

THE DYNAMO KIEV TEAM WERE *NOT* EXECUTED AFTER BEATING A GERMAN SS TEAM IN 1942

The so-called Death Match is perhaps the most mythologised game in football history. The story is that the Ukrainian team Dynamo Kiev played a Nazi SS team and beat them – and as a result they were all shot. No one is denying how evil the SS were, and what appalling war crimes they committed in Ukraine and other parts of the former Soviet Union. But this story simply isn't true. We want to believe it, because it *should* be true. Just as we want to believe Hitler snubbed Jesse Owens at the 1936 Olympics in Berlin. But he didn't.

On the contrary, a Ukrainian historian has shown that defeats of German football teams against Ukrainian clubs during the German occupation happened regularly. The Ukrainian press, controlled by the Germans, published many reports about these matches. The results of 111 games that are known are that the Ukrainians won 60 and lost 36, and 15 were drawn.

The Kiev city team FC Start, which represented the city's Bread Factory No. 1, was composed mostly of former professional footballers from Dynamo Kiev and Lokomotiv Kiev who worked at the factory under the occupying Germans. Seven FC Start matches are documented for June and July 1942, two against Ukrainian teams, three against Hungarian military teams, one a team of the German artillery and one a German railway team. FC Start won all the matches, scoring 37 and conceding only 8 goals. In August 1942, FC Start beat a German team 5-1. In front of 2,000 fans, the teams met again three days later, in what would become known as the Death Match. The poster advertising the game stated that the Germans had a 'strengthened' team. But the match ended 5-3 to FC Start. After the match, a German took a photograph of both teams, showing a relaxed atmosphere.

Ten days later, FC Start beat another German team 8-0. It appears that, angered by this humiliating defeat, the opposition coach denounced the FC Start team to the Gestapo and eight were arrested and questioned. After three weeks in a Gestapo prison, eight of the former Dynamo players were deported to a concentration camp and forced to work, both inside and outside the camp. Six months later, three of them were executed at the camp; however, this does not appear in any way to be linked to the football matches, but to incidents at the camp. Indeed, after the war the Soviet authorities punished some of them for collaborating with the Germans, which may simply have been because they had played football against them.

So how did the myth come about? It's largely Soviet propaganda. The expression 'Death Match' first appeared in the newspaper *Stalinskoye plemya* ('Stalin's tribe') in August 1946, when a film script of the events was published. In 1958, two novels about the Death Match were published. These inspired a film, *The Third Time* (1962), which was seen by around 32 million people in Soviet cinemas. The Death Match was also a very popular subject in the Soviet press. None of these publications mentioned any survivors of the match.

The reports about the Death Match changed in the mid-1960s. Under Soviet leader Leonid Brezhnev, the propaganda of the Communist Party had to highlight the heroism of the Soviet population during the Second World War. The Death Match became part of Kiev's heroic war history. The exact number of victims was given: four Dynamo players were murdered by the Germans.

In 1965, the Supreme Soviet of the USSR posthumously awarded four FC Start players killed by the Germans the 'Medal for Courage'. Five surviving players got the 'Medal for Battle Merit'. Despite a KGB dossier warning about the 'glorification' of the players with apparently 'known' collaborators among them, two monuments to the team were erected in Kiev in 1971. The Zenit Stadium, where the match had taken place in 1942, was renamed the FC Start Stadium. The Western media has since swallowed the Death Match myth because we want it to be true, it should be true, and also – why let the truth get in the way of a good story?

17

2-0 IS *NOT* THE WORST LEAD

It's a widely held belief of football fans that a 2-0 lead is the most dangerous winning margin. Fans think that if their team has a two-goal lead they will become complacent and are more likely to concede a draw, or even lose, than if their team is just 1-0 up. The team concentrates better and fights harder when there is only one goal in it. But this simply isn't true.

There is clear evidence from the Premier League: 2,766 teams have held a two-goal advantage during a game since the Premier League started in 1992. Of those, 2,481 ended up winning the match, an overwhelming 90 per cent. Only 212 ended in draws and 73 – just 2.6 per cent – ended up losing.

Teams with a one-goal advantage are far less likely to win. Of the 5,721 sides that have been one goal ahead during the Premier League era, only 2,987 (52.2 per cent) won the game, 1,747 drew and 987 lost – almost one in five. So a 1-0 leading margin is much more vulnerable than a 2-0 lead. A team that goes 2-0 ahead has actually increased its chances of winning by almost 40 per cent – that is, from 50 per cent to 90 per cent! A 2-0 lead away from home is only marginally less advantageous than a 2-0 home lead. The odds on a comeback from such a deficit are remote at best, and shrink as the match progresses, to less than 1 per cent if you go 2-0 down with only half an hour to go.

So why do fans believe this myth? We tend to remember the times when that lead collapses and forget the far more numerous times when our team led 2-0 and won. If anything, fans are just as superstitious about a 3-0 lead, especially if their team is 3-0 up at half time! They recall 'many' games where their team, or other teams, have drawn or even lost after being 3-0 up, because they relaxed too much, and the opposition, which now had nothing to lose, went for it. But this is even less true! Since the beginning of the Premier League, 1,119 teams have led by three goals and 1,099 of those claimed all three points, which is a 98 per cent win rate. In 25 years, only 16 teams have fought back from three goals down to secure a draw and just 4 have overturned the deficit to win, which is 0.4 per cent. Only one team in the entire Premier League era has come back to snatch a draw after falling four goals behind. Arsenal squandered a 4-0 advantage after 68 minutes against Newcastle in February 2011 to end up drawing 4-4 at St James' Park.

Fans remember those very rare amazing comebacks and forget the times when their team was 3-0 down, and lost 3-0 or 4-0 or 5-0! Instead, we remember when Liverpool, 3-0 down at half time in the 2005 UEFA Champions League final, fought back to 3-3 in the second half, and then won on penalties. Perhaps the most extraordinary comeback in the Premier League came in September 2001, when Manchester United trailed Tottenham 3-0 at half time away and came back to win 5-3. In 2012, Reading were 4-0 up against Arsenal in a League Cup match but somehow managed to lose 7-5 after extra time! In 2001, in an FA Cup fifth round game, my team, Tranmere Rovers, then in the Championship, and at home, were 3-0 down to Premier League Southampton at half time, only to win 4-3. But of course, I don't remember all the times we were 3-0 down – and lost!

These comebacks are the wonderful exceptions. So forget your superstition – 2-0 up and you are likely to win more than 9 times out of 10. 3-0 up, and its 98 per cent in your favour. Try and do something that no football fans can ever do – relax!

18

MOST FOOTBALL MANAGERS MAKE *NO* DIFFERENCE AT ALL

Football managers, as at no point in the game's history, are now celebrities that transcend the sport, such as Sir Alex Ferguson, José Mourinho and 'Pep' Guardiola. There were managers in English football before this who were famous – think of Sir Matt Busby, Bill Shankly, Brian Clough – but not at the level of global fame of today's managers. Today, football managers have cult-like status. We think these great names, these great characters, make the difference between success and failure. In the past, when clubs were fairly equal in financial resources, they may have done. But now it's largely a myth. Most football managers make *no* difference at all.

Herbert Chapman effectively invented the modern role of the manager, and in doing so made Huddersfield Town in the 1920s and then Arsenal in the 1930s the most successful clubs in England, winning two Football League Division One championships and one FA Cup at each club. Chapman changed the existing role of the manager, which was little more than an administrator to the board of directors of a club, to that of tactician and dealer in the transfer market. But once other clubs saw the value of such a role, this initial advantage diminished.

The simple fact is that in modern football it's all about the money. The richer the club, the more it has to spend on buying the best players and paying the top wages to attract these players. Statistically, the more a club spends on wages, the more successful it will be. The correlation between wages and league position in the Premier League and the Championship is as high as 87 per cent in one study, 92 per cent in another, leading to a conclusion that it's around 90 per cent. It's as simple as that. That leaves the manager's role as able to explain only up to a 10 per cent difference – better or worse – to this. Of course, there will be variations from season to season, there is no guarantee each season that wages will dictate league position. Sir Alex Ferguson at Manchester United and Pep Guardiola at Manchester City have had relatively bad seasons. This is down to luck, good or bad, with the likes of injuries and refereeing decisions. But over a few seasons, the higher the wages, the greater the success will be, as long as the manager is basically competent.

While the ability to pay higher wages will always have been a factor, it was much less so in the past, which means the manager previously had more impact. There was a maximum wage for footballers in England until 1961, and though some clubs got around this with 'extra' payments to players, broadly this meant there was a level playing field among the top 30 or so clubs in England. Managers then could make a real difference, such as Herbert Chapman and Sir Matt Busby at Manchester United. Even after the maximum wage was abolished, the top 20 or so clubs could still compete fairly equally for the top players from the 1960s to the 1980s, which meant the manager still made a significant difference. This is the era of the likes of Bill Shankly at Liverpool, Don Revie at Leeds, and Brian Clough at Derby County and Nottingham Forest. But since 1992, in the Premier League era, the gulf between the top six clubs and the others in terms of their financial resources has grown exponentially, and so even the best manager at a poorer club struggles to succeed. As we have seen, Ranieri at Leicester City was a one-season exception.

So where does this leave the cult of the manager? Yes, some are better than others. But the best managers, who also tend to be at the best clubs as these can pay the highest manager's wages too, can only add a few percentage points in the modern game. Sir Alex Ferguson would not have succeeded at Manchester United if it did not have the money to pay such high wages to players. Let's remember, he was nearly sacked after his first few seasons with the club. His success there is in large part down to his ability to attract the best players by being able to pay top wages, something that was challenged towards the end of his time at United, by Chelsea and then Manchester City. His successor, David Moyes, might have been the 'new' Sir Alex, given time. He signed a six-year contract in August 2013, and won the FA Community Shield in his first official game in charge, making him the first United manager in history to win a trophy in his first season. But he also had a lot of bad luck in his first season. Luck evens out over two or three seasons, but the modern game at the highest level needs instant success, and Moyes was sacked after just 10 months, with United seventh in the table. Moyes's record was second only to Sir Alex in terms of win percentages, better than Sir Matt Busby. Statistically, he was given far too little time to prove himself.

More significant than the success a manager can bring in the modern game is the failure he can bring through a poor transfer policy, simply buying the wrong players. In six seasons at Liverpool, Rafael Benítez spent a net £78 million on transfer fees and didn't win the league. In the same period, Arsène Wenger made a net surplus on transfers at Arsenal of £27 million and didn't win the league either, while Sir Alex spent a net £27 million at Manchester United and won three Premier League titles. However, during this period United were spending the most on players' wages, so of course they should have had the greater success!

So it's largely about the money. Most managers, assuming basic competence, do *not* now make much, if any, difference. A few, like Sir Alex Ferguson, do add something special, but there are very few of his calibre, to make a real difference.

19

DENIS LAW'S BACK-HEEL GOAL FOR MANCHESTER CITY DID *NOT* RELEGATE MANCHESTER UNITED

27 April 1974. Manchester United's Old Trafford stadium. It's one of the most iconic moments of football. Manchester United legend Denis Law brilliantly back-heels a winning goal *against* Manchester United, and Manchester United as a result are relegated. And Law is playing for … Manchester City. Except it's not true. His goal did not relegate United. They were going to be relegated anyway.

Scotsman Denis Law began his career at Huddersfield Town in the English Second Division in 1956. In 1960 he was signed by First Division Manchester City for £55,000, a new British record. A year later, City sold him to Italian club Torino for £110,000, then a record for a transfer involving a British player, but a year after that Manchester United bought him for another British record fee of £115,000. At United he became a legend, not just in England, but across Europe. The former Dutch striker Dennis Bergkamp (born 1969) is named after him! As part of the so-called Holy Trinity, with George Best and Bobby Charlton, Law scored an incredible 237 goals in 404 appearances, winning the league twice, the FA Cup, the European Cup and European Footballer of the Year in 1964. In the summer of 1973, aged 33, Law was given a free transfer by United to arch-rivals Manchester City.

The 1973–74 season was a mediocre one for City, finishing 14th, but Law scored a respectable 12 goals in 29 appearances. But United struggled very badly, and when they came to play Manchester City in their penultimate game, City's last game of the season, they were in a relegation spot. They needed at least a draw against City, and then a win against Stoke City in their last game on 29 April, and for Birmingham City to lose their last game.

At Manchester United's Old Trafford stadium, in front of a crowd of 56,000, after 81 minutes the score was 0-0. Then came Law's back-heeled goal. And for the first time in his career, this legendary goal scorer did not celebrate. As he said later, 'I just felt depressed, and that wasn't like me. After 19 years of trying my hardest to score goals, here was one that I almost wished hadn't actually gone in. I was inconsolable. I didn't want it to happen. How long did the feeling last? How long ago was the game? Thirty-odd years. There is your answer.' But note the goal scorer's overriding instinct here – he could only say he *almost* wished he hadn't scored! Law didn't know it at the time, but his goal made no difference – Birmingham City were beating Norwich City, so even a draw was not enough to save United. If Law didn't know this, the United fans did. They immediately invaded the pitch, a number of pitch invasions followed, Law was substituted, further pitch invasions followed, and four minutes later the referee was forced to abandon the game. After a review, the Football League decided that the result should stand. But United had already been relegated.

This goal should not be remembered as the one that relegated Manchester United, because it didn't. It should be remembered as the last goal scored by a legendary striker. After playing one last time for Scotland, in the World Cup finals game against Zaire in June 1974, in August 1974 Law retired from football. What a brilliant – but poignant – last goal.

20
WOMEN'S FOOTBALL IS *NOT* NEW

Football has been perceived as a man's game – and many men in the game in the past, and still today, would like to keep it that way. To some extent, football (like many sports) was invented and has existed to *exclude* women, whether as players or spectators – it came into being to be an exclusively male activity. The widely held perception is that women have recently begun to play football in increasing numbers, and today the vast majority of football fans are at least aware that there is a FIFA Women's Football Cup.

However, women have been playing football from almost the beginning, and indeed even before Association football started in 1863. Women have always resisted football being defined as a male sport. In England, women were playing 'folk' or 'street' football from at least the time of Queen Elizabeth I. In 1580, English aristocrat and poet of renown Sir Philip Sidney wrote the following, in 'A dialogue between two shepherds': 'Tyme there is for all, my mother often sayes, when she, with skirts tuckt very hy, with girles at football playes.' We know that women played even earlier versions of football, such as the ancient Chinese game of cuju, as early as 200 BC.

In 1895, a leading campaigner for votes for women in England, Lady Florence Dixie, organised a British Ladies Football Match between the 'North' and 'South' of England. This was political propaganda – the argument was that if women could play football like men, then they should have the vote like men. The North won 7-1, which perhaps was no surprise, as the north of England dominated men's football at this time, as it has for much of the following 125 years. Until recently, this was thought to be the earliest women's Association football match, but historians have now found records of games played in both England and Scotland in the early 1880s, although it's most probable Scottish women were the first to play Association football. Evidence has also now been found that Britain's first recorded international women's football match took place in Edinburgh in May 1881, when a team from Scotland beat one from England 3-0. Women's football appears to have continued in the UK, but on a relatively small scale, until the First World War. As Trotsky said, 'War is the locomotive of history', and women's football grew on an unprecedented scale during the First World War. As men were conscripted into the armed forces, women took up their jobs in industry, including in munitions factories, and took up playing football to raise money for disabled servicemen and the widows of servicemen and their families. The games they played came to draw crowds of over 10,000.

The women's game grew even more in popularity after the war ended, with crowds of up to 53,000, leading in part to the FA's attempt to quash the game in 1921 (see Chapter 33). Though this was a blow, the women's game continued, and there were internationals with Belgium, France and others. There was a big revival in the 1960s and 1970s in England, in other parts of Europe and the USA, in part linked to the rise of feminism. The growing popularity of women's football and pressure by women led to the first FIFA Women's World Cup in 1991 and the first Olympic women's tournament in 1996. The women's game is now firmly established in many countries. But women have had to fight all the way against sexism for the right to play and to be treated with respect, on a par with the men, and there is still a long way to go. Women fans have equally had to fight for respect, dignity, and even toilets, for most of the game's history. The game should be 50 per cent female – let's make it happen.

21

PENALTY SHOOT-OUTS
ARE A LOTTERY

Penalty shoot-outs *are* a lottery. They didn't used to be, although they were at first. Let me explain. Before the penalty shoot-out, drawn ties were decided by the toss of a coin or the drawing of lots. In 1970, a proposal by FIFA's Referees' Committee for a fairer method was accepted by the International Football Association Board (IFAB), and the penalty shoot-out was introduced in June of that year. In England, the first penalty shoot-out in a professional match took place in August 1970 between Hull City and Manchester United, during the semi-final of the Watney Cup, and was won by Manchester United. The first player to take (and score) a kick was George Best, and the first to miss was United's Denis Law.

At first, neither team practised for penalties, which meant that it was a lottery, but also for a second reason, as I will explain later. Then some teams got wise and practised for penalty shoot-outs, which gave them an advantage, thus removing part of the chance element. This is in part why England historically had such a bad record in penalty shoot-outs; they didn't practise, while some other countries – especially the Germans – did. As the then England manager, Bobby Robson, famously said before the World Cup in Italy in 1990, penalties are just a lottery. Whereas the Germans knew that if you practised, and your opponents didn't, then you could tilt the odds in your favour. West Germany beat England in a penalty shoot-out in the semi-final.

When Sven-Göran Eriksson became manager of the England team in 2001, he was shocked to find this lack of practice for penalty shoot-outs was still the case – which might explain our loss against Germany in the UEFA Euro '96 semi-final on penalties. Today, the England team practises penalty shoot-outs, and they managed to beat Colombia in the World Cup in Russia in 2018 – England's first win in a World Cup penalty shoot-out. But no doubt the Colombians also practised.

It's now a lottery again, if both teams practise equally well, because there is another chance element in penalty shoot-outs that has been there from the beginning, and at present is still there – though it could change. When both teams didn't practise, or now when both teams do, this remains a big, if not the biggest element of chance in a penalty shoot-out, favouring one team over another even before a single penalty has been kicked. The alternating kick sequence used gives an unfair advantage to the team kicking first, with statistical evidence showing that the team kicking first wins 60 per cent of the time, almost certainly due to the team kicking second being under more pressure when trailing in the shoot-out. So the teams taking the first penalty on average have a very significant in-built advantage. Which team takes the first penalty is chosen by the toss of a coin – pure chance.

As a remedy, it has been proposed instead to use the Thue-Morse sequence to determine the kicking order. As part of a trial to reduce this advantage, in March 2017 the IFAB sanctioned a test of a different sequence of taking penalties, known as 'ABBA' – yes, seriously – that mirrors the serving sequence in a tennis tiebreak (team A kicks first, team B kicks second), as follows:

- Original sequence: AB AB AB AB AB (sudden death starts) AB AB etc.
- Trial sequence (Thue-Morse sequence): AB BA AB BA AB (sudden death starts) BA AB etc.

The trial was initially scheduled at the 2017 UEFA Men's and Women's Under-17 Championships if a penalty shoot-out was needed. The trial was extended to include the 2017 UEFA Men's and Women's Under-19 Championships. The penalty shoot-out in the Women's Under-17 Championship semi-final between Germany and Norway was the first ever to implement this new system. The Germans won 3-2, but after missing their first three penalties! They scraped a win because Norway missed four of theirs. England won the Men's Under-19 tournament – but thankfully without the need for ABBA penalties (though presumably they had practised).

This new method was also used in the 2017 FA Community Shield in August 2017. This match, between Arsenal and Chelsea, ended 1-1 after 90 minutes. The penalty shoot-out that then followed was the first time the ABBA system was trialled in English football. Chelsea were drawn as A, Arsenal as B. Cahill took the first penalty for Chelsea and scored, and then Walcott and Monreal scored for Arsenal, before Chelsea goalkeeper Courtois kicked his penalty over the bar and Morata of Chelsea saw his go wide. Arsenal's Oxlade-Chamberlain converted his and then Giroud scored for Arsenal, to give Arsenal a 4-1 win in the shoot-out. There was no need for Chelsea to even take their fourth penalty, they had already lost. So the team taking the first penalty had lost – on this occasion. The Thue-Morse sequence (though ABBA is a catchier name), if rolled out from this trial, should even out this major chance factor, which would mean that on average penalty shoot-outs will no longer be a lottery – if both teams practise!

22

IT WILL *NEVER* BE A GLOBAL GAME – EUROPEAN COUNTRIES WILL INCREASINGLY DOMINATE THE WORLD CUP

FIFA proudly tells us that it has 211 member nations, more than the United Nations. FIFA quite rightly seeks to develop the game around the world, and despite some problems with corruption, largely does a good job in helping to develop the game at a grass-roots level, especially in poorer countries, where help is needed most. But this is not going to translate into more nations outside Europe challenging to win the men's World Cup. The opposite is going to happen – Europe is going to increasingly dominate the World Cup, to the point where a non-European country may not win it for the next generation.

A myth developed that European countries could not win the World Cup in America, and South American countries struggled to win in Europe. This stemmed from the fact that of the first 16 World Cups, from 1930 to 1998, the brilliant Brazil side of 1958, with Garrincha and the 17-year-old Pelé, was the only one to win on another continent. The first World Cup held in Asia in 2002 was won by Brazil, and Spain won the first World Cup in Africa, in South Africa in 2002, but the first European team to win a World Cup in the Americas was Germany in 2014. The 2006 and 2018 World Cups were won by European teams in Europe. In total, European teams have won 12 World Cups, South American teams have won 9. Europe has provided 28 of the finalists, South America 14 – with none from any other continents. So Europe has led historically, but not dominated.

The failure of teams playing in other continents historically has been put down to climate, altitude, food, culture, travel and coming across playing styles that were very different, which in the past led to violent encounters between South American and European teams in World Cups, such as the 'Battle of Santiago'. This was a group match during the 1962 FIFA World Cup, between hosts Chile and Italy. In an incredibly violent game, two players were sent off, numerous punches were thrown and police intervention was required four times. The referee was the Englishman Ken Aston, who later went on to invent yellow and red cards, perhaps inspired by this game! They would have been useful. BBC TV sports commentator David Coleman described it as 'the most stupid, appalling, disgusting and disgraceful exhibition of football, possibly in the history of the game' – that is, the kind that most fans secretly really enjoy!

But there are other, more significant factors to explain why teams have struggled on other continents. Such as simply not turning up. Most of the top European teams refused to go to the First World Cup in Uruguay in 1930. Many South American teams, including Uruguay, boycotted the 1934 and 1938 World Cups, and some European teams declined to go to Brazil in 1950 – including Scotland. Travel is now much easier, players are much better prepared, they acclimatise very carefully. Players often play in the same team as players they face at the World Cup, or play against them in European leagues or European club competitions, and tactical styles are now much more similar. Playing on different continents is no longer a big issue.

However, the last four winners have been European. In Russia in 2018, both finalists were European, all four semi-finalists, six of the quarter-finalists, and ten of the last 16. This is despite Europe having only 14 of the qualification places. Only four European teams failed to qualify from the group stage, and one of these was, very surprisingly, Germany. Europe also dominated in terms of the players at the tournament, in that 544 of the 736 squad members of all the countries competing – that is, 74 per cent – play in European leagues.

So Europe dominated the 2018 World Cup. And it will continue to do so. This is despite the 2026 World Cup being extended to 48 teams, which will give more places to Africa and Asia. There will just be more non-European teams going home early. In the current FIFA World Rankings (April 2019), eight of the top 10 are from Europe, and the other two from South America. Of the top 20, 14 are European, five South American, and one Central American (Mexico). The highest African team is Senegal (23rd). The highest Asian team is Iran (21st). Of the top 50 teams, 29 are from Europe. Europe only got 14 places at the 2018 World Cup. On the quality of the teams, it should have got much more.

Europe will increasingly dominate. European leagues will have more of the top players from around the world. Europe has the financial resources to nurture and develop young playing talent, and to take that talent from countries around the world. Most South American, African and Asian countries simply don't have the money. A great Brazilian team might win the World Cup again at some point, but a North American, Central American, Asian, African or Australasian team will not. Europe will provide most of the quarter-finalists, semi-finalists, finalists and winners of the next five World Cups at least.

23

HOOLIGANISM IS *NOT*, AND *NEVER* HAS BEEN, A MAJOR PROBLEM IN ENGLISH FOOTBALL

Beginning in the 1960s, England gained a reputation worldwide for football hooliganism; the phenomenon was often dubbed the 'English disease'. But it's a myth. It just wasn't that significant.

I am not saying that football hooliganism wasn't and isn't a problem, just that in the scale of problems in society, its importance has been grossly inflated. How many people have died as a result of football hooliganism in England? The answer is probably one. Yes, one. Yes, hundreds of people have been injured, some of them seriously. But in terms of fatalities? In 1982, after a derby match between Arsenal and West Ham United, a supporter was stabbed and killed in a riot between fans of the two teams. In 1985, a 14-year-old boy died at Birmingham's St Andrew's stadium when fans were pushed by police on to a wall, which subsequently collapsed, following crowd violence at a match between Birmingham City and Leeds United. Arguably, this tragic death was not as a direct result of football hooliganism. The boy did not die by the act of another person, but as a result of a wall collapsing. Was the wall fit for purpose? So in fact there appears to have been only one death as a direct result of football hooliganism in England.

There have been 185 deaths at football matches in England; however, these were not caused by hooliganism, but by the inadequate condition of the stadiums and poor crowd control. These are the tragedies at Burnden Park, Bolton, in 1946, when 33 fans died as a result of overcrowding and poor crowd control; the fire at Valley Parade, Bradford City's stadium, in 1985, which killed 56 people; and at Sheffield Wednesday's Hillsborough stadium in 1989, when 96 Liverpool fans died. In each case, the fans were the victims, not the cause of these tragedies. Indeed, the fans at Hillsborough may well not have died if there had not been perimeter fencing around the pitch, which had been put in place at most grounds to prevent 'hooligans' invading the pitch. As Lord Justice Taylor said in his report on the disaster: 'Prison-type fences with spikes with overhanging sections should go.' The Bradford City fire was on the same day as the death of the 14-year-old boy at Birmingham. In the case of

Hillsborough, the fans were blamed by the police and the media, and the victims' families and their supporters had to fight for nearly 30 years to clear their names and bring to justice those who were responsible for this tragedy. The fight goes on, with finally the possibility of legal action against those who may have been responsible.

What of the terrible reputation of England fans abroad? The only incident that led to fatalities was in May 1985, when 39 Juventus fans were crushed to death during the European Cup final between Liverpool and Juventus at Heysel Stadium in Brussels, an event that became known as the Heysel Stadium disaster. Just before kick-off, Liverpool fans broke through a line of police and ran towards opposing supporters in a section of the ground containing Italian fans. Many fans tried to escape the fighting, and a wall collapsed on them. As a result of the Heysel Stadium disaster, English clubs were banned from all European competitions until 1990, with Liverpool banned for an additional year when other English clubs were readmitted. It was not until 1995 that England got all of its European places back. While the actions of the Liverpool fans in charging at the Juventus fans was shocking, and 14 were convicted, they did not set out with the intention to kill. Had there been proper segregation of fans, control by the police, and had the stadium been fit for purpose, the disaster need not have happened.

Football hooliganism was completely exaggerated by the media and the establishment. The government set up a 'war cabinet' in 1985 to combat football hooliganism. The fighting at the game between Birmingham City and Leeds United was described by Justice Popplewell, during the Popplewell Committee investigation into crowd safety at sports grounds in 1985, as more like 'the Battle of Agincourt than a football match'. This was an utterly ridiculous thing to say, demonstrating the establishment's hysteria at the time. One boy tragically died in Birmingham. Thousands died at Agincourt in 1415.

I am not saying that a minority of fans do not sometimes behave badly – very badly – both at home and abroad. Hooliganism was and still is a stain on the game. While there appears to have only been one death as a direct result of football hooliganism, there have been many injuries, and at times an unpleasant if not downright scary atmosphere created for the vast majority of fans by the hooligans. Again though, we need to keep this in perspective. Fans know to stay away from the pubs and other gathering places of the hardcore hooligans. Sensationalist media reporting has over-stated the problem. Media footage of drunken English 'fans' chucking plastic chairs at 'fans' from other nations in squares in cities overseas during World Cups and the Euros, being water-cannoned and charged at by riot police, have come to be seen as the norm, rather than the exception.

As someone who went to football throughout the 1970s and 1980s, I knew how to avoid the trouble. I was more concerned about violence in any English city centre on a Saturday night – or down in a Tube station at midnight. Football hooligans then – and now – largely fight each other, often in prearranged locations away from the ground. Innocent bystanders sometimes get caught up in it, but largely could and can avoid it. It has been a problem, it's still a problem, but it must be kept in perspective. And it should not be called, as we shall see in chapter 34, the 'English disease'.

24
FOOTBALL SHIRT COLOURS *DO* MATTER

The colour of your sports kit *does* matter. There is scientific evidence that wearing red is an advantage in sport – and this includes football.

Sports psychologists at the University of Münster showed video clips of taekwondo bouts to 42 experienced referees. One combatant wore blue, the other red. They then showed them the same clips but digitally manipulated the clothing to swap the colours. The fighters wearing red were given an average of 13 per cent more points than when they wore blue. 'If one competitor is strong and the other weak, it won't change the outcome of the fight', said Norbert Hagemann, who led the study. 'But the closer the levels, the easier it is for the colour to tip the scale.'

In 2004, researchers at Durham University also looked at how colour influenced sporting competitiveness. They analysed Olympic combat sports such as boxing, taekwondo, Greco-Roman wrestling and freestyle wrestling, and found that nearly 55 per cent of bouts were won by the competitor in red. They found that there is now 'good experimental evidence that red stimuli are perceived as dominant... It is plausible that wearing red also makes individuals feel more confident, although this hasn't yet been tested.'

So does this also happen in football? England's victorious World Cup team in 1966 wore red, instead of their usual white, and have not won a World Cup or European Championship since! An academic study has found that since 1947, English football teams wearing red shirts have been champions more often than expected on the basis of the proportion of clubs playing in red. This could simply be due to the success of a couple of teams who (mostly) wear red, Liverpool and Manchester United, so the research went much further. They analysed the relative league positions of teams wearing different colours. Across all league divisions, red teams had the best home record, with significant differences in both the percentage of maximum points achieved and the average position in the league table. The effects were not due simply to a difference between teams playing in a colour and those playing in a predominantly white kit, as the latter performed better than teams in yellow kits.

A matched-pairs analysis of red- and non-red-wearing teams in seven English cities shows significantly better performance of red teams over others in a 55-year period.

So it does seem to be that wearing red in football is also an advantage. But why? Perhaps the biased perception of the officials, as demonstrated in other sports. Or teams wearing red may be perceived as more attractive to paying supporters, due to their success, indirectly due to the psychological association between success and the colour red. With more fans attracted, this brings greater financial resources to winning clubs over time. However, this phenomenon may have changed recently, with a shift in the main source of finance at major clubs from fans to individual wealthy benefactors. The injection of large sums of money into individual teams, irrespective of shirt colour, may begin to override any selective advantage that red as a colour has built up over the last 70 years or so. So maybe Manchester City in blue will continue to be more successful than Manchester United in red, as they have been for the last few years. Maybe the days of a slight advantage to red in football is over?

25

AFRICA IS *NOT*, AND *NEVER* HAS BEEN, A FOOTBALL BACKWATER

Most football fans outside of Africa think that the sport has only developed there in recent years and that, apart from developing a few great players, African football is fairly primitive, because of the relative poverty of the continent. Our view of football in Africa is coloured by our wider misconceptions of the continent. However, football is by far the most popular sport in Africa and is also probably the most popular sport in each country. And it has a very long history too. Africa is not, and never has been, a football backwater.

Football was first introduced to Africa in the late 19th century by Europeans, spreading very quickly through the mission schools, the military forces and the railways. The two oldest surviving clubs began playing football in South Africa and Egypt in 1882. By the 1930s, football was being played in central Africa. The Confederation of African Football (CAF) was founded in 1957, only three years after UEFA. The first Africa Cup of Nations was held the same year, three years before UEFA's first European Championship finals. The CAF Champions League for clubs (the equivalent of the European Cup) was first held in 1964.

The first African nation to participate in the FIFA World Cup was Egypt in 1934. In a knock-out match they lost 4-2 to a very strong Hungarian team. For the 1938 World Cup, Egypt were drawn to play a qualifier against Romania but were unable to play as it was during Ramadan, so FIFA awarded the place at the World Cup to their opponents. Egypt failed to qualify for the 1954 World Cup, after losing in qualification home and away to Italy. The odds at this time were strongly stacked against African qualifiers by FIFA. Both African nations that applied for the 1958 World Cup, Egypt and Sudan, were made to compete in an Africa/Asia zone with 10 Asian countries for just one spot at the World Cup. Sudan defeated Syria 2-1 on aggregate but withdrew in protest at having to play Israel. Eventually, the spot originally reserved for Africa and Asia was taken by Wales. Seven African countries entered the qualification process for the 1962 FIFA World Cup, but group winners Morocco were forced into a play-off game with Spain, and lost.

Seventeen African countries entered the qualification process for the 1966 FIFA World Cup, two of which were rejected. FIFA's allocation of only one place to three continents (Africa, Asia, Oceania) was subject to significant criticism, especially given the large increase in applications from newly independent African countries. After FIFA confirmed the allocation, the remaining 15 African nations withdrew in protest. This poor treatment of African (and Asian) countries was one of the main reasons why English FIFA president Sir Stanley Rous lost to the Brazilian João Havelange in the election for FIFA president in 1974.

While club football is popular across Africa, drawing large crowds, one of the key issues is the exodus of players to play in European professional football, drawn not least by the much greater wages on offer. African players *have* become global superstars, but by moving to Europe, and then very often qualifying to play for a European nation. Eusébio is a classic example. Born in the then Portuguese colony of Mozambique in 1942, he moved to Portugal in 1960, won the European Cup with Benfica in 1962, was European Footballer of the Year in 1965 and was the star of the 1966 World Cup. Since then, some outstanding

African players have played for the country of their birth, such as Didier Drogba, Samuel Eto'o, Yaya Touré and Mohamed 'Mo' Saleh. George Weah was FIFA World Player of the Year in 1995 – and is now the President of Liberia. African football has been a key part of football's history, and is a major part of the game today. But rather than having to play in Europe, we need to see a time when the top African players can play in Africa, for clubs that can compete with the best in the world.

26

ENGLISH FOOTBALL HAS *NEVER* BEEN CLEAN, CHEATING HAS ALWAYS BEEN PART OF IT

We have seen the highly dubious way Arsenal got into the top flight of English football in 1919, and how its chairman was later found guilty of corruption. But this scandal is far from exceptional. English football history is littered with acts of cheating, bribery and corruption. English football has *never* been clean.

The British pride themselves on being a nation with very limited corruption, a nation that likes to play fair, at work and at play, especially in sport. The British sense of fair play and sportsmanship extends out of sport into all aspects of life, and indeed these values came from the British public schools of the Victorian era. In these elite, fee-paying schools, sport taught the boys values for life. Many of the older generation in Britain still use the phrase 'that's just not cricket' if something is seen not to be fair. And it's true that in international indexes of corruption in business and public life, Britain comes out well. But of course there is and always has been corruption in Britain, and despite these notions of fair play, sport has not been immune. Fair play as taught in the Victorian public schools was, after all, reconciled with ruthlessly creating and maintaining the British Empire, which the boys at the public schools were being trained to run.

We think that, compared with many other countries, English football is and has been clean and fair, but it hasn't. There have been major scandals and crimes in football around the world, but British football has not been any cleaner, far from it. The phrase is 'That's not cricket', not 'That's not football'! Indeed, there have been innumerable scandals in British football, from the beginning, including outright cheating, bribery and match-fixing. Unless these issues have come to court, we have remained unaware. Some of them have only come to light decades later, when the evidence emerges, or someone finally owns up to having fixed a match. Ever since football became professional and money was at stake, people have tried to make money corruptly out of the game.

Simon Inglis's great 1985 book *Soccer in the Dock: A History of British Football Scandals 1900 to 1965* is full of extraordinary tales of corruption and malpractice – after reading it, you wonder if you can ever trust a football result again. To take just one example from a great many, the fixture on Good Friday of 1915 between Liverpool and Manchester United was judged to be fixed, which caused embarrassment to two of the biggest clubs in England. The match, which ended 2-0 in United's favour, helped them avoid relegation and in the process got Chelsea relegated. However, the match referee and some observers noted Liverpool's lack of commitment during the game. They had missed a penalty that had been awarded to them, and when Fred Pagnam hit the Manchester United crossbar late in the match, his teammates publicly remonstrated with him. Players from both United and Liverpool were involved, and four from United and three from Liverpool were banned for life after the FA investigation found them guilty. However, rumours persisted that it was not just the players who were involved, but that the chairmen of Liverpool and Manchester United were leading this – but they got away with it.

But that was all in the past, wasn't it? There have been plenty of additional scandals and scares since then, it is a continuous history, and given the vast amounts of money now in British football, it has perhaps become a more major problem. The range of corruption and scandal in British football includes: players having drink, drug and gambling problems; cheating on their wives and girlfriends; players, club owners and referees fixing games for money and/or betting on the games; directors stealing from the club; managers and players taking a cut of transfers; players being involved in assaults and affray; players being accused of sexual assault and even rape; players caught drink-driving; the role of the players' agents; tax avoidance and evasion. Much of what has gone on in football in financial terms over the last 20 years or so has not been illegal, but very often clearly immoral and unethical, as David Conn has exposed in detail in his books *The Football Business: The Modern Football Classic* and *The Beautiful Game? Searching for the Soul of Football.*

So can we trust football, even in Britain? The authorities will say, unequivocally, yes – there are too many checks and balances for anyone to get away with cheating. And that, for example, players will no longer be tempted to fix a match for money, because they already earn so much. But of course only a small proportion of players have big earnings, and even the wealthiest players can, and have, got into financial difficulties, which has left them open to corruption.

Criminal betting syndicates have been seeking to influence even the outcome of Premier League games. For example, in November 1997 Crystal Palace were playing West Ham at Upton Park and Frank Lampard had just equalised for the home side when the stadium suddenly went dark. The floodlights had failed and the game had to be abandoned. As the east London fans trudged home early, on the other side of the world, in Malaysia, members of an Asian betting syndicate were congratulating themselves on a six-figure win. The syndicate orchestrated a repeat performance a month later, when the lights blew as Wimbledon faced Arsenal, but they failed to pull it off a third time during a Charlton versus Liverpool game. A security guard had been paid to fuse the lights, but he let details of the arrangement slip to a co-worker, who informed the police. The Charlton security supervisor, a Chinese man and two Malaysians subsequently received prison sentences of between 18 months and four years. Players at lower league clubs are still being caught in betting scandals.

No, British football is not 100 per cent clean, despite the best efforts of the football authorities. But the two biggest and most damaging scandals in British football have not been about money. They have done far greater harm than stealing cash can ever do. These scandals are the appalling treatment of the 96 Hillsborough disaster victims and their families, from the day of the disaster itself, through the smears, the cover-up, right up to the present day, and the continued fight for justice. The other is the appalling paedophile sexual abuse scandals that have rocked English football since 2016, the dreadful damage that has been done to the victims and the failure over decades by the football authorities to identify and prevent this abuse. Justice for Hillsborough and for the sexual abuse victims, and to ensure that tragedies such as these never occur again, is the biggest challenge facing the English game.

27

ENGLAND IS *NOT* THE CENTRE OF FOOTBALL, AND FOR MUCH OF ITS HISTORY IT'S BEEN A BACKWATER

For much of football's history, English football – club and country – has been of marginal importance to the world game. Despite what the English think. Yes, the English invented the modern game in 1863 – but the Scots (and Welsh and Irish) immediately had a major input. In international football, Scotland were much better than England up to 1914. The English Football League, begun in 1888, led the way, but the Scottish Football League, founded in 1890, was also very successful. Englishmen (but also Scots, Welsh and Irish) took football overseas, founding clubs. For example, in 1891 Herbert Kilpin became the first Englishman to play abroad and was one of the key founders of Milan Foot-Ball and Cricket Club (later AC Milan) in 1899. But other nationalities were just as important in spreading the game to other countries. The virus of football had already spread from England, or rather from Britain, across Europe, on railway lines. It was no longer under British control. For example, FC

Barcelona was founded by the Swiss sportsman Hans Max Gamper, also in 1899.

In the 1920s and 1930s the English Football League was still admired in Europe, but the major tactical and technical innovations were already taking place elsewhere, especially in Austria and Hungary. This was compounded by the British football nations leaving FIFA in 1928 and refusing to play in the first three FIFA World Cups, in 1930, 1934 and 1938. The British nations rejoined FIFA in 1946, but only England went to the World Cup in Brazil in 1950, where they lost ignominiously to the USA, then lost to Spain and were eliminated at the group stage. In 1953 England were tactically humiliated by Hungary at Wembley by 6 goals to 3, and then crushed 7-1 by Hungary in Budapest the following year. A home win in the World Cup in 1966 masks a very poor record for England in other World Cups, with only two semi-final appearances, being knocked out in the group stages four times, and even failing to qualify for the finals in 1974, 1978 and 1994.

While a number of English clubs won the more minor European club competitions – that is, the Fairs Cup (later the UEFA Cup) and the Cup Winners' Cup – Manchester

United's victory in 1968 was the first English win in the European Cup, which began in 1955. The second came from Liverpool in 1977 and was the first of a remarkable sequence of seven wins in eight years by English clubs (Liverpool, Liverpool, Nottingham Forest, Nottingham Forest, Liverpool, Aston Villa and Liverpool). But after that there was no English winner until Manchester United in 1999, and there have only been four since. Spain has had 18 winners compared with England's 13.

The Premier League may be seen by millions around the world on TV, but much of this is because it has attracted players from 107 countries, and fans in these countries are watching *their* best players playing in England. The Premier League is undoubtedly a major global football brand, but it's arguably English in name only, as 69 per cent of the players are not British. The Bundesliga and La Liga have a majority of home-grown players. The Premier League also fails to attract the very top players. In the history of the Premier League, the only Ballon d'Or winners at English clubs have been Michael Owen in 2001 and Cristiano Ronaldo in 2008. Even when the top players have had a spell in the Premier League, they have played their peak years elsewhere, such as Cristiano Ronaldo, Luis Suárez, Gareth Bale and Luka Modrić. Some of the greatest stars of the world game, like Messi and Neymar, have never played in the Premier League. The Premier League has put English football back on the world stage in the last 15 years or so, though not necessarily through the quality of the football, and up until then, globally English football was largely only remembered as history.

28

THE GERMANS DO *NOT* ALWAYS WIN ON PENALTIES

It's become one of the great quotes of football. According to England football legend Gary Lineker, 'Football is a simple game. Twenty-two men chase a ball for 90 minutes and at the end, the Germans always win on penalties.' When Germany scored a late winning goal to stay in the 2018 FIFA World Cup, after they had had a player sent off, Lineker had a new version: 'Football is a simple game. Twenty-two men chase the ball for 82 minutes and the Germans get a player sent off, so 21 men chase the ball for 13 minutes and at the end the Germans somehow fucking win.'

But it's not true. The Germans might have beaten England in two key penalty shoot-outs – the World Cup semi-final in 1990 in which Lineker played (and scored his penalty) and the European Championship semi-final at Wembley in 1996 – but the Germans do *not* always win on penalties.

For a start, the Germans only win 50 per cent of penalty shoot-outs – in their domestic football! The

Germans have no better a record than anyone else at club level in European competitions. And the last time there was an England versus Germany penalty shoot-out of some kind, in the 2012 Champions League final, Chelsea beat Bayern Munich.

It's in international football that there is the perception that the Germans always win on penalties. In fact, the Germans only have a 60 per cent win percentage – six wins, four defeats. Fifteen teams have better records. England have won two and lost seven. This makes England one of the worst performers in international football. In the UEFA European Championship, the Germans have won two but lost one. The Czech Republic, Spain and Turkey have better records. England have won one and lost three.

It's at the World Cup where Germany has the best record. But of course, this is a very small sample size – they have been in four and won all four. England have won one and lost three. There are very fine margins at this level. But nine other teams also have a 100 per cent record, from winning the one or two shoot-outs they have been in in World Cups. The Germans don't think of themselves as invincible, especially after the farce of the European Championship penalty shoot-out against Italy in 2016. Germany eventually won 6-5 on penalties, despite missing three of their first five spot kicks – by Müller, Özil and Schweinsteiger! Both teams were extraordinarily inept.

So while England think this of Germany, the Germans don't think this of themselves, and it isn't true. So why do we think it? The defeats by Germany in 1990 and 1996 were particularly hard to take, as on both occasions, in open play, England had been the better team. The Germans have won the key ones, those in the World Cup, and lost others. But England have lost the key ones, only having won against Spain in the quarter-final of UEFA Euro '96 and Colombia in the World Cup last 16 game in 2018. The Germans aren't that great at penalties, but the English, until 2018, were terrible.

So this is about our attitude to the German football team, and a sense of inferiority that we seem to have in relationship to them. Not surprising, since England has only won the World Cup once and the Germans have won it four times. Germany has replaced Scotland as England fans' greatest football rival. But England are not Germany's, so it's one-way. England beat Germany 5-1 in a World Cup qualifier in 2001, and England fans and the English media went crazy. The DVD (or was it video back then?) sold by the bucketful. But what happened then? Both teams qualified for the 2002 World Cup. England lost in the quarter-finals. Germany lost in the final. England need to forget about the Germans, and just get good at penalties!

29

HOME ADVANTAGE IS *NOT* AS VITAL AS WE THINK – AND ITS VALUE IS DECLINING

Yes, playing at home is still an advantage. But it's *not* as vital as we think – and its value is declining. But why is it falling? And why exactly is it an advantage in the first place?

Home advantage has been on a steady decline since the Football League began in 1888. At its peak in the 1895–96 season, home teams won 64.6 per cent of their games. Home win percentage hit an all-time record low in 2015–16, down to just 41.0 per cent across the four English divisions – the Premier League, Championship, League One and League Two. That same season, away wins hit an all-time high, at 31.5 per cent. The long-term trend is a move away from draws towards away wins. Both Premier League home and away goals are increasing over time – with the sharpest increase coming in away goals.

It's not the same in each English league. Home advantage is greatest in the Premier League, with a win percentage of 49 per cent, which falls to 40 per cent in

League Two. International football has a higher home win percentage. An analysis of nearly 9,000 international matches between 1993 and 2004 found that international home sides won 50.5 per cent of games, with the away team winning 24.5 per cent, and 25 per cent finishing as draws. Studies have also found that football has the largest home advantage of any sport. On average, since 1992–93 the home team scores around 1.53 goals compared with 1.12 for the away team.

So why are away teams performing increasingly better? Tactical developments mean that teams playing at home and away increasingly approach the game differently. Sides no longer employ the same tactics away as they do at home, where the emphasis is on them to attack. Away from home they now often choose to sit deep, stay compact and counter-attack when the home team overcommits. They pick different sides away from home, to reflect this.

But why is there any home advantage at all? The home advantage seems to disappear when a team moves stadium. In 2016–17, West Ham relocated to the Olympic Stadium and dropped from a 0.34 of a goal home advantage in the previous four seasons to a –0.63 of a goal disadvantage. This was effectively an entire goal swing caused from moving grounds, and their home advantage being eradicated. So maybe the stadium is part of it.

The home crowd does seem to have an impact. A study of 5,000 Premier League games from 1992 to 2006 found that for every 10,000 home team fans, home advantage increased by 0.1 goals. But it's not the supporters intimidating the away team. The research found that inexperienced referees were more likely to award penalties to the home team. There is overwhelming evidence that referees' decisions are biased towards the home team, indeed that referees are the most influential factor in home advantage, and that home teams gain a small bias from referees who are affected subconsciously by the emotion of the home crowd. Research has even suggested that the longer and louder the home crowd boos and appeals, for example, for a red card or a penalty against the opposition, the more likely a referee is to comply with their wishes. This is why home advantage is greater in the top leagues than lower down the divisions, with their smaller crowds. Between 1992 and 2014, penalties in the Premier League led to goals 85 per cent of the time. Of these 1,666 penalties, almost two-thirds – 63 per cent – were awarded to the home team. Research in the German Bundesliga found that home advantage was smaller in stadiums with a running track surrounding the pitch than those without a running track, as the crowd was less able to intimidate the referee. So what every fan has ever thought about referees is true!

Other researchers have looked at games played in Italy in 2007. Following several clashes between hooligans and police, clubs were ordered to play matches behind closed doors if they could not provide adequate security. This resulted in 21 matches being played with no crowd at all for the rest of the season. The results were fascinating. Despite the absence of a crowd cheering them on, players performed much the same. They had the same shots on target percentages, the same passing accuracy and even the same amount of tackles were made. No difference. But the pattern of refereeing decisions changed. The away team was penalised for fouls 23 per cent less than they usually would be, were awarded 26 per cent fewer yellow cards and 70 per cent fewer red cards. So your team does need you to be vocal – both home and away!

30

IT'S SCIENCE, *NOT* ARTISTRY, THAT MADE THE BRAZILIANS THE BEST AT FOOTBALL

Whenever Brazil are at the FIFA World Cup, all the lazy stereotypes of Brazil, and Brazilian football, come out in the English media, and not just the tabloid newspapers. This still happened during the 2014 World Cup in Brazil. Brazil is a huge country, but to the British media it's very small. It's the Copacabana beach in Rio de Janeiro, where both British TV companies had their pundits' studios in 2014 (though in fairness FIFA located them there), with Sugarloaf Mountain in the background, even though England weren't actually playing in Rio. The simple British media formula is Brazil equals Copacabana beach, equals samba music, equals naturally talented young boys playing football on the beach and growing up to be the new Pelé. Behind this lies a lazy, racist stereotype, which is that Brazilians, especially black Brazilians, are somehow naturally talented at football, they have natural 'samba' gifts to dribble balletically with the ball, which they don't really need to practise. But unlike the (white)

Europeans, they aren't any good at defending, at tackling and heading. While we are increasingly moving away from this prejudiced view, as most of the Brazilian team are now very well known to us as they play in Europe, it's still there, and this stereotype was stronger in the past.

We believed that Brazil were so good at football, and kept winning the World Cup, because they were somehow more naturally gifted. Which is, of course, complete nonsense. From time to time Brazil has produced some exceptionally talented players, such as Pelé. But so have we. They haven't won five World Cups by being good at the samba, but by hard work, practice and, crucially, the appliance of science – before most of the Europeans.

The man behind this is now one of the most disgraced figures in world football history, João Havelange, who was president of FIFA from 1974 to 1998. In July 2012, a Swiss prosecutor's report revealed that, during his tenure on FIFA's Executive Committee, Havelange and his son-in-law were paid 41 million Swiss Francs in connection with the award of World Cup marketing rights. But Brazil's football success owes much to Havelange.

Havelange was the eldest son of wealthy Belgian immigrants who settled in Rio de Janeiro early in the 20th century and made money from arms dealing. Havelange wanted to become a professional footballer, but for someone from his social background this was not acceptable – sport should be amateur. Havelange pursued swimming and competed for Brazil in the 1936 Olympics in Berlin, and at the next Olympics in Helsinki in 1952 he was in Brazil's water polo team. He then went into sports administration and by 1958 he was president of Brazil's sports federation, which at the time included Brazilian football and its national team. He held this post until 1973, during which time Brazil won the World Cup three times.

Brazil had failed in the first five World Cups, most notably in 1950. Even today, deep in the Brazilian national psyche – despite five World Cup wins since! – is the scar of Brazil's highly unexpected (by Brazilians) defeat in the deciding match in the 1950 World Cup against Uruguay in the Maracanã Stadium, in front of 200,000 fans, known as 'El Maracanazo', 'the Maracanã blow'. In 1954, an ill-disciplined Brazil lost 4-2 to the great Hungarian team in the quarter-final match, dubbed the 'Battle of Berne', with two Brazilians sent off. Brazil did not expect to win in Switzerland in 1954 – no team had won on another continent in the first five World Cups – but Brazil's failure in 1950 had to be expunged.

Havelange didn't know much about football tactics, but his organisational skills were supreme. While preparations for earlier World Cups had been amateurish, the squad that travelled to Sweden for the 1958 World Cup was perhaps the best-prepared national team in history to date. Nothing was left to chance. Brazil had a thorough training schedule before the tournament. With the players and manager in Sweden was a backroom team that included coaching staff, a doctor, a dentist and a psychologist. Brazil asked that female staff at their team hotel be replaced with men, so the players would not be distracted. Before the final against hosts Sweden, Brazil even complained about the Swedish cheerleaders, and these were banned from the game. Brazil, inspired by a hat-trick by a 17-year-old Pelé, won 5-2, and became the first team to win the World Cup on another continent.

The same scientific approach, together with talented players, ensured Brazil's victory in 1962. By comparison, England's approach at this time was amateurish. The team was chosen by a selection panel rather than the coach, Walter Winterbottom. An English woman was found in Chile to cook English food for the players.

In 1966, in England, referees failed to protect Pelé from being fouled and he was kicked – literally – out of the tournament. In 1970, Havelange made sure that Brazil's preparation for the Mexico World Cup was even more meticulous. The team was together for three months before the tournament. The training programme used techniques developed by NASA, including altitude training. Brazil triumphed in 1970 not because they had the best eleven players, but because they had the best preparation.

Others still failed to understand this. A very well-known, very influential and at the time globally recognised English soccer writer (who will remain nameless) wrote before the 1970 World Cup that Brazil's emphatic qualifying victories against Venezuela meant nothing, as 'I cannot help feeling that a team drawn from the Cumberland town my family comes from would give Venezuela a good run'. He added that Brazil had 'a grossly overrated midfield pair in Gerson and Rivellino; talented yes, but so eager to show off their ball skill they seldom bothered to look about and play off the first-time ball'. Further, he said he 'cannot agree that the Brazilians have modified their game, for the fans of Rio de Janeiro and São Paulo have always regarded football as we look upon a circus – an arena in which talented jugglers show off their unusual skills'. Finally, Brazil were 'disorganised but talented', and so would not win in 1970. All stereotypes that Brazil were no doubt pleased to read, as it gave them a further edge.

Having been instrumental in leading Brazil to three World Cup triumphs, Havelange challenged the Englishman Sir Stanley Rous to be elected president of FIFA in 1974 – and won. He prepared brilliantly for this election. Again, Brazilian planning had defeated English 'amateurism'. Havelange's meticulous planning and scientific approach ensured Brazil won three World Cups – *and* effectively took control of FIFA for the next three decades.

31

THE WORLD CUP HAS *ALWAYS* BEEN CONTROVERSIAL

Awarding the World Cups to Russia in 2018 and Qatar in 2022 have been seen as highly controversial choices, with accusations of corruption in the process, and that the politics of these two countries did not make them appropriate hosts. But regardless of the rights and wrongs of Russia and Qatar, the FIFA World Cup has *always* been mired in controversy and corruption allegations.

Uruguay seemed a natural choice to host the first World Cup finals in 1930, as the highly convincing winners of the Olympic football tournaments in 1924 and 1928, and with the country due to celebrate the centenary of its first constitution, from 1830. However, the cost and time needed to send a team by ship from Europe meant that only five European teams were convinced by FIFA president Jules Rimet to take part, despite Uruguay offering to contribute to travel expenses. As a result, the tournament had only 13 participants out of a possible 16. The Uruguayans built a new stadium to host the major matches in the tournament, the 90,000-capacity Estadio Centenario (Centenary Stadium). It was the largest football stadium outside the British Isles at the time. However, in a major embarrassment for the organisers, it was not ready for use until five days into the tournament, and thus the first two matches had to be moved to a smaller stadium in Montevideo. The final was between hosts Uruguay and neighbours and arch-rivals Argentina. The teams could not agree which ball to use, as the ones they each commonly used had different designs and colours, so they used a different ball in each half! An Argentinian ball was used in the first half and at half time Argentina led 2-1. A Uruguayan ball was used in the second half and proved lucky for them – they scored three and won 4-2.

Mussolini did everything he could to ensure Italy won the 1934 World Cup, which was held in Italy. Mussolini clearly expected victory, as he commissioned a second, unofficial, winner's trophy, the 'Coppa del Duce', which was six times taller than FIFA's Jules Rimet trophy! After a lengthy decision-making process in 1932 in which FIFA's Executive Committee met eight times behind closed doors, Italy was chosen as the host nation, without a ballot. The Italians bent the rules of the time by using several 'oriundi', South Americans of Italian ancestry. Since they were eligible for military service, the Italian coach Pozzo's logic was 'if they can die for Italy, they can play for Italy', although when Italy entered the war in 1940, some of the oriundi were caught trying to get across the border into neutral Switzerland. In the finals, it seemed the referees strongly favoured Italy in wins over Spain and Austria. The referee for the final was the man who had taken charge at Italy's semi-final against Austria, and one of his linesmen was the referee who had so favoured Italy against Spain. It is widely believed that the refereeing appointments were now being made by Mussolini himself and that the referee for the final dined with Mussolini the evening before the game. Critics felt the referee again favoured Italy in the final, as they beat Czechoslovakia.

The 1938 finals were in France, so Mussolini could not fix them, but he sent a telegram to the Italian team, which read 'Vincere o morire!' – 'Win or die!' The 1938 World Cup was heavily marred by international politics. Spain became the first country to be prevented from competing, due to its civil war. Austria had officially qualified for the finals, as had Germany, but because of the Anschluss (the annexation of Austria by Nazi Germany in March 1938), the Austrian national team withdrew, with some Austrian players being added to the German squad. Germany went out after losing 2-4 to Switzerland. This loss, which took place in front of a hostile, bottle-throwing crowd in Paris, was blamed by German coach Sepp Herberger on a defeatist attitude by the five Austrian players he had been forced to include. A German journalist later commented that the 'Germans and Austrians prefer to play against each other even when they're in the same team'. With the success of the football tournament at the 1936 Olympics in Berlin, Germany applied to host the 1942 World Cup. If the Second World War had not started, Nazi Germany would probably have held the next World Cup.

We have already seen how the 1966 World Cup in England was marred by controversy. Worse was to follow with the 1970 World Cup qualifications. El Salvador qualified for the finals after beating Honduras in a play-off match, which was the catalyst for a four-day conflict in July 1969 known as the Football War, in which over 2,000 people were killed. There was a military coup in Argentina in June 1966, so it was not a democracy when it was chosen as the host for the 1978 World Cup. The country remained politically unstable until a further coup in 1976. Under this murderous new regime, thousands of people were imprisoned, killed, or simply 'disappeared'. Controversially, all Argentina's games in the first round kicked off at night, giving the Argentines the advantage of knowing where they stood in the group. Further accusations surround the game Argentina and Peru played in the second round of the tournament. Argentina needed to win by a margin of four goals to proceed to the final and did so by defeating Peru 6-0. There was an alleged deal, reported by the British media, that involved the delivery of a large grain shipment to Peru by Argentina and the unfreezing of a Peruvian bank account held by the Argentine Central Bank. When Argentina won the final, political prisoners were let out for the evening by their guards to celebrate. However, a guard warned: 'If you try to run we'll put a bullet in you. With all the fireworks, no one will notice.'

Spain was under the dictatorship of Franco in 1966 when it was awarded host status for the 1982 World Cup. It only made the transition to a democracy in 1977. The 1986 World Cup was marred by perhaps the ultimate problem – the withdrawal of the host country. The Colombian authorities announced in November 1982 that they could not afford to host the World Cup under the terms that FIFA demanded, because of political and financial turmoil and the emergence of powerful and ruthless drug cartels. The United States, Canada, Brazil and Mexico all offered themselves as replacements for Colombia, but the decision was ultimately between the Americans and Mexicans, the latter having hosted the tournament as recently as 1970. The Americans, backed by Pelé and Franz Beckenbauer, appeared to have the most influential support. However, Guillermo Caneda, the head of Mexican media giant Televisa, was a FIFA vice-president and was apparently able to persuade the then president of FIFA, João Havelange (who was later disgraced for receiving money), that his commercial blueprint – including the inflated sale of television rights to European broadcasters – would transform FIFA's finances. Mexico's staging of the tournament just 16 years previously was conveniently overlooked.

When we look back at World Cup history, nothing that happened in Russia in 2018 or will happen in Qatar in 2022 has or will come near to what has happened at many previous World Cups, in terms of controversy and corruption allegations...

32

THERE *ARE* GAY FOOTBALLERS – AND THERE ALWAYS HAVE BEEN

There are no 'out' gay players in the English Premier League. But of course there *are* many gay and bisexual players in it. There have been rumours for a number of years that up to 20 current Premier League players were considering coming out, but were concerned about prejudice and a hostile reaction from fans. So, at present, top-level players only feel comfortable to come out after their career has ended. Liam Davis, a semi-professional player, remains the only current male player to have come out during his paid playing career in English football.

This is different in top-level women's football, where many of the England team have come out, including the current captain, Steph Houghton. But women players have only felt comfortable to do this in recent years. Casey Stoney made 130 appearances for England between 2000 and 2017, was appointed captain in 2012 and also became captain of the newly formed Team GB squad for the 2012 London Olympics. She was appointed as the first head coach of the newly formed

Manchester United Women club in 2018. Yet she didn't feel comfortable enough to come out until towards the end of her playing career, in 2014. Historians have suggested that Lily Parr, the greatest English woman player of the 1920s and 1930s, and the first female player to be inducted into the English National Football Museum Hall of Fame, was openly lesbian during her playing career. In many countries, lesbian, gay, bisexual and transgender (LGBT) people face legal punishments and even imprisonment, and so cannot even consider coming out. In 2011, the Nigerian women's football team said that it had successfully banned homosexuality among players.

There have, of course, always been LGBT footballers, right from the very beginning of the game. But as the game began in the very socially conservative Victorian English society, with strong prejudice, and even the law against LGBT people, this is a very hidden history. There was great prejudice against *women* playing football in Victorian England! So it is very unlikely that we will ever know who the LGBT football pioneers were.

Justin Fashanu, the first black £1 million footballer, was the first professional footballer to be openly gay, not just in England, but globally. He faced appalling prejudice from his manager at Nottingham Forest, Brian Clough. Fashanu scored the BBC *Match of the Day* Goal of the Season in 1980 for Norwich City, but his career faltered after his move to Nottingham Forest, no doubt as a result of both racist and homophobic abuse. Fashanu came out as gay in the media in 1990. Tragically, he committed suicide in 1998, aged just 37. He had been questioned by police in the USA when a 17-year-old boy accused him of sexual assault. The coroner said the prejudices he experienced, plus the sexual assault charge he was facing at the time of his death, probably overwhelmed him. Justin's experience is probably why no other player in England has come out since. Globally, it remains very difficult for male – professional and amateur – players in particular to come out, even in supposedly liberal, tolerant societies, so only a very small number of professional players have, perhaps as few as seven. Some players, like Thomas Hitzlsperger, have only felt able to come out after their retirement from the game.

Robbie Rogers's story shows just how hard it is for professional footballers to come out, but also how inspirational he has been. In 2013 American player Rogers came out as gay, being only the second professional player to do so after Justin Fashanu – 23 years earlier. Rogers began his professional career in the Netherlands in 2006, before returning to Columbus Crew in Major League Soccer (MLS) in 2007, with whom he won the MLS Cup in 2008, and he made 18 appearances for the USA from 2009 to 2011. He had a brief, but largely unsuccessful spell with Leeds United in England from 2011 to 2013. Weeks after being released by Leeds, Rogers announced his retirement from professional soccer at the age of just 25 and came out, on his blog, writing 'I'm a soccer player, I'm Christian, and I'm gay. Those are things that people might say wouldn't go well together. But my family raised me to be an individual and to stand up for what I believe in… Life is simple when your secret is gone. Gone is the pain that lurks in the stomach at work, the pain from avoiding questions, and at last the pain from hiding such a deep secret.' In his first interview, with the UK's *Guardian* newspaper in March 2013, he was asked if he could ever see football's last taboo being overcome: 'Yes. I know things will change. There will be gay footballers. I just don't know when and how long it will take. The next step is how do you create an atmosphere where men and women feel it's OK to come out and continue to play? It's a great question.' Asked if he would play professionally again, he said, 'I've thought about that. I might be strong enough but I don't know if that's really what I want. I'd just want to be a footballer. I wouldn't want to deal with the circus. Are people coming to see you because you're gay? Would I want to do interviews every day, where people are asking: "So you're taking showers with guys – how's that?" If you're playing well it will be reported as: "The gay footballer is playing well." And if you have a bad game it'll be: "Aw, that gay dude … he's struggling because he's gay." Fuck it. I don't want to mess with that.'

Rogers had secured a place on a three-year course at the London School of Fashion. Just a few weeks later he changed his mind. He spoke to a group of about 500 kids at the Nike Be True LGBT Youth Forum in Portland, USA. 'I seriously felt like a coward. These kids are standing up for themselves and changing the world, and I'm 25, I have a platform and a voice to be a role model. How much of a coward was I to not step up to the plate?' The following month Rogers became the first openly gay player in the MLS when he played his first game for LA Galaxy. After winning the MLS Cup in 2014, unfortunately Rogers's career was ended by injury in 2017. But not before he had been an inspiration to many young players.

It is appalling that LGBT players and fans still face prejudice, at every level of the game, and this needs to change. The football bodies must show leadership, but the fans have a key role to play in the professional game. There are positive signs. Along with Robbie Rogers, one of the most inspirational examples is that of Jaiyah Saelua, an American Samoan international football player and the first transgender player to compete in a men's FIFA World Cup qualifying game. Saelua identifies as fa'afafine, a third gender in Polynesian society. Saelua made 10 international appearances, and was part of the American Samoan team featured in the excellent documentary film *Next Goal Wins*. While an accepted part of Polynesian society, Saelua has faced prejudice playing teams from other cultures in international matches: 'I have been called names a few times just to put me off my game, but I just tackle harder.' Of course it's a long way from the American Samoan national team (FIFA ranking

190 as at April 2019) to the Premier League, but if Jaiyah Saelua can face the prejudice and tackle harder, here's hoping some Premier League stars will soon show the same courage. There will be prejudice, there will be hate, from a minority, but most fans I believe will be supportive, and indeed proud of the first players to come out.

33

THE FA DID *NOT* BAN WOMEN'S FOOTBALL IN 1921

The uncovering of this previously hidden history of women's football has led to a new myth. This is that women's football in England was getting so popular during and after the First World War, with crowds of up to 53,000 at games, that the FA banned women's football in 1921. The new myth is also that, as a result, women's football largely disappeared, until the FA overturned the ban after 50 years in 1971.

The problem with this is that it's not true. It's not even true that the FA banned women's football. The FA's statement on 5 December 1921 was:

Complaints having been made as to football being played by women, the Council feel impelled to express their strong opinion that the game of football is quite unsuitable for females and ought not to be encouraged.

Complaints have been made as to the conditions under which some of these matches have been arranged and played, and the appropriation of the receipts to other than Charitable objects.

The Council are further of the opinion that an excessive proportion of the receipts are absorbed in expenses and an inadequate percentage devoted to Charitable objects.

For these reasons the Council requests the clubs belonging to the Association refuse the use of their grounds for such matches.

So the FA didn't actually ban women's football or the use of club grounds for women's games, though it may be that behind the scenes it was made clear to clubs that though it was worded as a *request*, it was *effectively* a ban. But it wasn't simply sexism that led the FA to this position. It genuinely believed that there was corruption, in that too much of the money raised, which was supposed to be for charity, was being pocketed by the players and the organisers. The final straw for the FA was probably not women playing the game, but that the money raised at some women's games was also now openly being used not for charity but for *political* purposes, with women's teams playing benefit matches for striking coal miners.

It is this last factor that appears to have triggered the FA's resolution in December 1921.

Though it was probably a de facto ban from connection with the men's game, this didn't end women's football, and why should it have? These women weren't going to be silenced so easily! The most famous team at the time, Dick, Kerr Ladies of Preston, vowed: 'The team will continue to play, if the organisers of charity matches will provide grounds, even if we have to play on ploughed fields.' Some supporters of women's football welcomed the decision of the FA. 'Football Girl' wrote in her weekly column in the *Football Special* magazine: 'Women's footballers have at last been roused to the necessity of organisation if they are to carry on, and the FA ban, having made us independent of outside bodies, has given us the additional impetus that will probably make us organise ourselves far more thoroughly than we should have done if we had been in a half-and-half situation, neither definitely sure of having the FA's assistance and yet to a large extent relying on it.'

This led to the first meeting of the English Ladies Football Association (ELFA), which was held in Blackburn in December 1921. At the time there were around 150 ladies' football clubs in England, but representatives from just 25 clubs came to that inaugural meeting. However, 60 clubs sent delegates to the following meeting, which took place in Grimsby.

The ELFA issued a statement that argued: 'The Association is most concerned with the management of the game, and intend to insist that all clubs in the Association are run in a perfectly straightforward manner, so that there will be no exploiting of the teams in the interest of the man or firm who manages them.' The Association introduced its own set of rules and regulations, which included reducing the size of the pitch. It was also decided to use a lighter football, and referees of women's matches were given 'greater powers concerning the use of ball skills rather than brawn', to encourage skilful play.

Women's football simply moved – to rugby grounds, to recreation grounds. Yes, the FA's de facto separation of the women's game from the men's game had been a severe blow, and the women's game was not as strong again as it had been in 1920 and 1921 – but it didn't die. Dick, Kerr Ladies went on a highly successful tour of Canada and the United States in 1922! Women's football continued, and then revived significantly with the renewal of the fight for women's rights in the late 1960s and 1970s. The women's game is now stronger globally than it has ever been, but women continue to face prejudice, and still have to fight for their rightful place in the game. When will we see a female Premier League manager, a woman player as an icon like Messi, or a woman as president of FIFA?

34

FOOTBALL HOOLIGANISM IS *NOT* THE 'ENGLISH DISEASE'

Football hooliganism came to be known as the 'English disease'. But this is wrong. Football hooliganism started elsewhere and has always been much worse in other countries. Fighting at football has existed for most of its history. But this perhaps is inevitable to some extent, with crowds of thousands of people watching something they are passionate about, and fans of the other team in close proximity. Early instances in England date back to the 1880s, but tended to be attacks on referees, rather than the fans of the other team. But soon after football began in each country around the world, the problem also began to arise there.

However, many nations in Europe in particular have their own hooligan myth, which is that in the 1970s English football hooligans came over to Europe for competition matches between their clubs and European clubs, and terrorised them in their ground and in their cities. So they had to learn how to be hooligans, to fight back when the English came again. This is the equivalent of the myth that the 'English' brought the game directly to every country in the world. English hooliganism gives authenticity to hooliganism in that country. Their hooligans learned from England, the 'mother' nation of hooliganism! The truth is that football hooliganism in each country is as old as the game in each country, and it was not brought by the English.

Academic studies have found that football hooliganism is an issue in almost all European countries, but the nations with the biggest problems, apart from England, are Scotland, Italy, Germany, the Netherlands and Belgium. Different factors come into play in each country, such as religious sectarianism in Scotland and Northern Ireland, sub-nationalist politics in Spain, and historical regional antagonisms in Italy. Yet all seem to share the same pattern of development. First, sporadic violence directed mainly at referees and players, followed by a second stage involving violence between fans of the two teams in the stadium, together with attacks on the police and stewards, with a third stage of violence between rival fans outside the stadium, as security inside the grounds is tightened. Italy is arguably the worst country for football hooliganism in Europe, with the 'Ultra' gangs, many stabbings, a significant number of deaths and the suspension of all football in the country for a time in 2007 after the death of a policeman.

There is a much stronger case for calling football hooliganism the 'Argentinian disease'. The first recorded death from football hooliganism in Argentina was in 1922, when the fan of an away team drew a gun and shot and killed a home fan. After the final match of the South American Championship in 1924 in Montevideo, Uruguay, an Argentinian fan shot and killed a Uruguayan fan. In 1939, after a foul in a game between Lanus and Boca Juniors, both teams began to fight. Seeing this, the Boca Juniors fans tried to tear down the fence and invade the pitch, prompting the police to fire shots to disperse them, and two fans were shot dead. In 1946, an Argentinian club match was two goals each when the referee disallowed a goal for the home team, and then the away team scored. After 89 minutes, several home fans invaded the pitch, hit the referee and tried to hang him with his own belt from the crossbar.

By the 1950s, fans of major Argentinian clubs had organised hooligan gangs – two decades before English fans did. Between 1958 and 1985, there were 103 deaths related to football violence in Argentina. A 2002 investigation into football hooliganism in that country stated that football violence had become a national crisis, with about 40 people murdered at football matches in the preceding 10 years. In the 2002 season, there were five deaths and dozens of knife and shotgun casualties. At one point the season was suspended. In 2005, a footballer was shot and seriously wounded by a police officer when rival fans rioted during a match. During the 2010 FIFA World Cup in South Africa, Argentina fans from two rival clubs, who were both there to support their country, clashed in Cape Town, and a fan was killed. In total, there have been over 250 deaths in Argentina linked to football hooliganism since 1924.

Argentina is the worst country for football hooliganism, past and present. So let's never again call it the 'English disease', but also not the Argentinian. It's a global problem.

35

FOOTBALLERS SINGING THEIR NATIONAL ANTHEM *DOES* MATTER

How many times have you watched the two teams during their national anthems at a World Cup game and thought that the team singing the anthem with pride and passion – and actually knowing the words – looked like they were more likely to win? Usually, the England players mumble or just pretend to move their lips. Is it just that our players – like the English as a nation – are reticent to sing in public? When he was England manager at the 2014 World Cup, Roy Hodgson observed that it was common for players from other countries to show pride at representing their country by singing the national anthem: 'You very rarely play against opponents and they haven't got their hands on their hearts and singing their anthem as loud as they can.' So why didn't he get England's players to do this? England went out at the group stage. After all, football games are one of the few places where English men – as football fans – can sing together and show emotion in public! And even chant they love 11 other men! Does it matter if your team sings the national anthem? Surely it doesn't make any difference?

Sports scientists have now studied this and found that it *does* matter. First, scholars have shown that singing – including the singing of national anthems – has important psychological and social consequences. At a group level, evidence suggests that compared with people who participate in other group activities, those who participate in group singing are more cooperative on a subsequent task. Moreover, evidence indicates that group singing makes emotional experiences more positive and leads to a greater experience of connectedness and sense of belonging. It thus appears that, especially when it is done in a group, singing has a range of important positive psychological consequences for teams and their members, improving collaboration and performance. Beyond the general benefits of singing together, teams are also likely to derive benefits from singing national anthems, as they are an important strand of a nation's symbols, rituals and traditions, because they define a nation's identity. They are important in our national psyche.

Academics have specifically examined the link between passion displayed by team members during the singing of national anthems at UEFA Euro 2016 and team performance in the tournament's 51 games. The results showed that teams that sang national anthems with greater passion went on to concede fewer goals. Further, there was evidence that the impact of this passion on the likelihood of winning a game depended on the stage of the competition. In the knockout stage (but not the group stage), singing with greater passion was associated with a greater likelihood of victory. So Hodgson should have got his players to sing.

Before the current England manager, Gareth Southgate, hires Gareth Malone or another English television personality choir leader to teach the England squad how to sing the national anthem with passion and gusto, and to learn the words rather than just mumble and pretend to know them, there is a proviso. If they only show passion because they have been instructed to do so then this is unlikely to be a recipe for success. In short, you do not just have to sing like you mean it, you actually have to mean it. So the first step is to build a strong psychological bond among the players, but also to inculcate pride and patriotism in playing for their country. The way they then sing the national anthem with pride and passion would be an expression of this. Come on then, the England team – the first line is 'God save our gracious Queen!'

36

THE FIFA WORLD CUP HAS *NOT* ALWAYS BEEN THE MOST IMPORTANT INTERNATIONAL COMPETITION

International football started in 1872, so the FIFA World Cup can't always have been the most important international competition, as it didn't start until 1930 – and in fact, it didn't become the most important international competition until at least the 1950s, and possibly even later.

For the women's game, the Olympics as much as the FIFA World Cup has a very special place, with winning the Olympics being seen as equal to winning the World Cup. According to former England international Lucy Ward at the 2012 Olympics, 'If somebody said would you rather win Olympic gold or the World Cup, it would be equal.' And the fans seem to feel the same – crowds at women's Olympic tournaments tend to be as large as those at the women's World Cup. While women's football has a long history, the first women's FIFA World Cup was in 1991 and it was only allowed in the Olympics from 1996.

The first FIFA men's World Cup was not until 1930, so for the first 60 years of football the most important international competition was simply England against Scotland from 1872, and then the British Home Championship from the 1883–84 season. This was an annual competition between England, Scotland, Ireland and Wales. Scotland won the first four so can claim to be the Brazil of the 1880s! Even after the creation of FIFA in 1904, the British Home Championship remained the most important international football tournament.

From 1912, Olympic football began to challenge it. Contrary to a popular perception, certainly in the UK at least, that somehow football does not 'belong' in the Olympics, it was planned from the outset that men's football would be part of the modern Olympic Games. At the first Olympic Congress in Paris in 1894, the desire was expressed that 'athletics games (football, lawn tennis, real tennis, etc.)' feature in the Olympic programme. Eleven nations competed in Stockholm in 1912, with 25,000 watching Great Britain win the final. In Antwerp in 1920, 14 nations took part, and a crowd of 35,000 watched the final. In Paris in 1924 crowds were generally good, with four matches attracting more than 40,000 spectators. Gate receipts from the final alone contributed a twelfth of the Games' overall income. Uruguay became the first South American team to compete, joining 18 European teams, the USA, Turkey and Egypt. In terms of the number of participating teams, this would be the biggest international football tournament until the 1982 FIFA World Cup in Spain. Despite being South American champions, little was known in Europe about the Uruguay team. It was therefore a surprise, in Europe at least, when they dominated the tournament. In Amsterdam in 1928, some 17 teams took part, with Uruguay drawing with Argentina in the final in front of a crowd of 28,000 spectators and winning the replay, attended by a similar number. There were 250,000 applications for tickets for the final from across Europe.

However, as the Olympics only allowed amateurs to compete, in 1928 FIFA decided to launch a World Cup, open to professionals. Yet only 13 teams competed in the first World Cup in Uruguay in 1930. Despite the successful 1934 FIFA World Cup, it was clearly in the interests of both the International Olympic Committee (IOC) and FIFA that football be included in the Olympic Games in 1936, in part because of its income-generating powers, so a deal was struck over the payment of expenses to players. Before the tournament, the IOC forecast that football gate receipts alone would cover the costs of the 1936 Olympic Games as a whole. Despite the unexpected early exit of Germany, watched by Hitler, who had apparently never seen a football match before, the football tournament was a great success in terms of crowds and income. For the semi-finals, bronze medal match and final, all played at the Olympic Stadium in Berlin, there were crowds of 95,000, 82,000, 95,000 and 85,000 respectively. This success led Germany to immediately put in a bid to host the 1942 FIFA World Cup, although the tournament was ultimately cancelled due to the Second World War before a host country had been chosen. The London 1948 Olympics football tournament was a successful event, attracting 18 teams, good crowds and 60,000 fans at the final at Wembley.

Olympic football tournaments continued to draw very good crowds, but the profile of the tournament declined, as professionals were barred until 1992, and then only players under 23 were permitted, and since 1996, three players over 23 years old have been allowed per squad. However, communist countries fielded full strength teams from 1948 until 1988, under the guise that they were amateur, and dominated the tournaments. Even so, early World Cups were low-key events, and it was not until at least the 1958 World Cup in Sweden that we could say they had overtaken the men's Olympic football tournament in significance. And those who compete in modern Olympics football tournaments, in front of large crowds and global TV audiences, are just as passionate to win as those at the FIFA World Cup.

37
THE PRAWN SANDWICH BRIGADE IS *NOT* NEW

After a Champions League game at Old Trafford in 2000, Manchester United legend and then club captain Roy Keane famously attacked the 'prawn sandwich brigade' for not getting behind the team enough. Except of course he didn't say that – and middle-class fans are not new at football. But now in England, 'prawn sandwich brigade' is a derogatory term for people who attend football matches primarily to enjoy luxury boxes and corporate hospitality, rather than support a team or enjoy the sport.

Keane castigated those in the corporate hospitality areas in particular for not being vocal enough in their support, and at times too quick to criticise minor mistakes, during the Champions League game against Dynamo Kiev. (United won 1-0 to go through to the second phase). Keane did not refer to the prawn sandwich brigade – the media invented and popularised this term shortly after. What he actually said was:

Our fans away from home are as good as any, but some of them come here and you have to wonder do they understand the game of football? We're 1-0 up, then there are one or two stray passes and they're getting on players' backs. It's just not on. At the end of the day they need to get behind the team. Away from home our fans are fantastic, I'd call them the hardcore fans. But at home they have a few drinks and probably the prawn sandwiches, and they don't realise what's going on out on the pitch. I don't think some of the people who come to Old Trafford can spell football, never mind understand it.

But the prawn sandwich brigade were not new at football, they were there from the start. Not just in the gentleman amateur era, but once professional football had begun. In terms of social class, right from the start in 1888, crowds at Football League matches were predominantly drawn from the skilled working- and lower-middle classes. Social groups below that level were largely excluded by the cost of entry. In its early years, the Football League set the minimum admission price for an adult male at sixpence, which may well have been a rather cynical attempt to dissuade less affluent – and therefore supposedly more unruly – supporters from attending. Football was too expensive for the poorest in society right from the beginning. Nor are women fans new. A number of clubs concluded that men would be better behaved at games if there were women present, so in April 1885 Preston North End offered women free entry to home games. More than 2,000 women came through the turnstiles for that first game. In fact, free admission for women became so popular that by the end of the 1890s all the football clubs that had originally signed up to the scheme had withdrawn from it, as they felt they were losing too much money.

So despite the popularity of Nick Hornby's novel *Fever Pitch*, first published in 1992, which has sold over a million copies in the UK, and is credited by many as bringing middle-class fans to football, this is not true. Middle-class fans are not new; indeed, Hornby himself is an example of this – as a (very) middle-class boy. He was the son of Sir Derek Hornby, the chairman of London and Continental Railways, and Margaret Audrey, Lady Hornby. Hornby first went to a match in 1968. He does not believe that his book had any such impact, or that any book could. As he says, this theory assumes that, because *Fever Pitch* is a book, its success was due entirely to a middle-class readership, because somehow working-class people – especially football fans – apparently don't read! As Hornby states, the game has to an extent become even more middle-class in recent decades, but this has been largely due to another man – Rupert Murdoch, owner of Sky Sports.

38

THE CHINESE *DID* INVENT FOOTBALL

Fans around the world recognise that the English invented modern football, Association football. Yet many countries then claim to have invented *football*, in that they had an earlier version of the game, their own form of football. And it's true, there were many earlier football games around the world, going back thousands of years.

So who has the best claim to have invented 'football'? The English themselves have claimed this, with earlier versions of the game dating back to the Middle Ages. Complaints by London merchants led King Edward II of England to issue a proclamation banning football in London in 1314 because 'there is great noise in the city caused by hustling over large balls from which many evils may arise which God forbid; we command and forbid, on behalf of the King, on pain of imprisonment, such game to be used in the city in the future'. Playing football was seen as a distraction from practising archery, which was a mandatory occupation for every Englishman for much of the Middle Ages, because archers were so valuable in battle at this time. This led King Edward III and King Edward IV of England to ban football in 1349 and 1477 respectively. The latter stated that 'No person shall practise ... football and such games, but every strong and able bodied person shall practise with the bow for the reason that the national defence depends upon such bowmen'.

However, recent research has found that some of these supposed medieval English games were in fact almost certainly much later in origin, an invented tradition. For example, the Alnwick Shrovetide Football Match, a large-scale (150 a side) football match played annually in Alnwick, Northumberland, on Shrove Tuesday, is said to be medieval in origin, but the earliest definite reference to it is in 1762. The most famous of these Shrove Tuesday football games in England, at Ashbourne in Derbyshire, is equally said to date from the Middle Ages, but there is no record of it before 1667.

Earlier football in England had no structure, no formal rules. Many other cultures had football going back at least a thousand years, such as the native peoples of North America, including the polar regions. When the British arrived in Australia, they found that the native people had their own football games, collectively called *marngrook*. Norwegian Football Association visitors to the National Football Museum told me that the Vikings invented football, playing with the severed head of one of their enemies after a battle. South Korean FA visitors told me the same story a few weeks later. The ancient Romans and Greeks had ball games, but it is not clear that we can in any way call them a version of football.

From 1400 BC the people of Ancient Mesoamerica started playing a ball game, which had different versions in different places over time, and a more modern version of the game, *ulama*, is still played in a few places by the indigenous population. Later, stone ball courts were built, many of which survive. It appears, however, that the one part of the body that was not used in this game was... the foot.

The Italians have a better claim for inventing football, as *calcio fiorentino* (also known as *calcio storico*, 'historic football'), an early form of football that originated in 16th-century Italy. Once widely played, the sport is thought to have started in the Piazza Santa Croce in Florence. There it became known as the *giuoco del calcio fiorentino* ('Florentine kick game'), or simply *calcio*, which is what Italians call Association football. Calcio was highly organised, with a set number of players, a marked pitch, and officials – many of the features of the modern football game.

But just as the ancient Chinese seem to have invented everything, so they also have the best claim to have first invented an organised football game. This has, quite rightly, been recognised by FIFA. There were different versions of this ancient football game, called *cuju*, and the game evolved over time, beginning in military exercise in the third century BC. Cuju had a delineated pitch, a set number of players, clear laws, and at one point a league with professional players. It appears to have lasted until the 16th century. There were at times a small number of women players. There is an excellent museum of cuju, the Linzi Football Museum, in Zibo, Shandong province, where the game originated. In 2015, Xi Jinping, the president of China, visited the National Football Museum for England, of which I was then the director. My gift to the president was a copy of the first laws of Association football from 1863. His gift to me was a replica of a cuju ball, the *first* organised football game in the world.

39

WOMEN'S SOCCER HAS *NEVER* BEEN MORE IMPORTANT THAN MEN'S SOCCER IN THE USA

When we think of Association football in the USA we think of soccer, and we think of women's soccer in particular. This is not surprising. Women's soccer is very big in the USA. It has a long history, as in England, going back to the late 19th century, and there is a professional league. The USA women's international team has been one of the most successful, winning the first FIFA Women's World Cup in 1991. They won it again in 1999, 2015 and 2019. They are also the only team to have won the World Cup four times; in the four other World Cups, they finished second once and third three times. The Olympics is arguably equally important in the women's game. Here, the record of the USA women's team is even better. They won the first Olympic women's football tournament in 1996 and have won three of the other five tournaments to date. The USA women's soccer team is unarguably the most successful international women's team in history. The team's players have become celebrities, featuring in photo shoots, on cereal packets, as Barbie dolls. 'Soccer Mom' is a widespread term in the USA, referring to those mothers ferrying their daughters in particular to soccer practice. But soccer in the USA has always been, and still is, bigger among men than women.

Men's soccer was thought to have been brought to the USA by immigrants from Europe into Ellis Island in the 1860s, but recent research suggests New Orleans was more important in the early development of soccer, and it wasn't just the English that brought it, but Irish, Scottish, Italian and German immigrants. At first, the term 'Association football' rather than 'soccer' was widely used in the USA, and the American Football Association (AFA) was founded in 1884 – for soccer. Early soccer leagues in the US mostly used the name 'football' – for example, the American League of Professional Football (1894) and the National Association Football League (1895). Common confusion between the terms American football and Association football eventually led to a more domestic widespread use of the term soccer with regard to Association football. Originally seen as a British slang term for 'association', the use of soccer began in the late 1910s and early 1920s. A noticeable example was the American Soccer League (ASL), which was formed in 1921. The governing body of the sport in the USA, incorporated in 1914, did not have the word soccer in its name until 1945, when it became the United States Soccer Football Association. It did not drop the word football from its name until 1974, when it became the United States Soccer Federation, often simply referred to as US Soccer.

In the 1920s heyday of the American Soccer League, soccer was seen as widely popular, and considered to be the second most popular sports league in the United States, behind only Major League Baseball. The USA men's team reached the semi-final in the 1930 FIFA World Cup. In the overall tournament records, FIFA credited the USA with a third-place finish, ahead of fellow semi-finalists Yugoslavia.

US men's club soccer declined sharply after the Wall Street crash in 1929, for both economic and organisational reasons, but did not die out completely. Operating from 1968 to 1984, the North American Soccer League (NASL) was the top-level major professional soccer league in the United States and Canada. It was the first soccer league to be successful on a national scale in the United States. The league's popularity peaked in the late 1970s, averaging over 13,000 fans per game in each season from 1977 to 1983, and its matches were broadcast on network television from 1975 to 1980. The league's most prominent team was the New York Cosmos. During the mid- to late 1970s, the Cosmos signed a number of the world's best players – Pelé, Franz Beckenbauer, Carlos Alberto – and the crowds averaged over 28,000 per game for each season from 1977 to 1982, with three seasons when the average attendance topped 40,000 fans per game. Other internationally well-known players in the league included Johan Cruyff, Johan Neeskens, Gerd Müller, George Best and Rodney Marsh. Though the league went into decline and ended in 1984, it had shown that the game had great appeal, partly because of its long and significant history in the USA, and had sown seeds for the future.

Hosting the men's FIFA World Cup in 1994 gave a major boost to soccer in the USA and a new men's league, Major League Soccer (MLS), was founded in 1993 as part of the United States' successful bid. MLS experienced financial and operational struggles in its first few years, but now it's a great success, with 21 teams in the USA and three in Canada. The USA men's team then also shot up the FIFA rankings and reached the quarter-final of the World Cup in 2002. The men's league draws much larger crowds than the women's league, and there are also more men playing the game than women. In 2016–17 there were 450,000 males and 388,000 females in high school soccer programmes. The USA may be the strongest nation for women's football, but men's soccer has always been bigger in the USA.

40

IT WILL *NOT* BE TOO HOT TO PLAY FOOTBALL IN QATAR

After Qatar was awarded the 2022 FIFA World Cup in December 2010, many in England in particular reacted negatively, saying it would simply be too hot. This was despite the Qatari bid specifying that all the stadiums, for both players and fans, would be cooled to between 24°C and 28°C (75–82°F). This would be cooler than at many, if not in fact most, previous World Cups! The then chairman of the English FA, Greg Dyke, said it would be 'dangerous' because 'you can have air-conditioned stadiums but you've got to get in and out of the stadium, and that can take you an hour. In that sort of heat it's quite dangerous I think.' This is despite the fact that people have lived in the Middle East for thousands of years and that it was the cradle of civilisation!

This view also ignored the fact that the Qatari bid said a summer World Cup was possible, but a winter World Cup was preferable. It ignored that Qatar had successfully held a number of major international sporting events, including the 2006 Asian Games (the second largest multi-sport event after the Olympic Games), the 2011 Pan Arab Games, most of the matches at the 2011 Asian Football Confederation Cup, and had bid for the Olympics. But the English football bodies did not want the tournament moved to the winter, as it would disrupt the Premier League season. This conveniently ignored that some Premier League teams, including Manchester United, have had winter training breaks in Qatar and for many years the English football bodies have been considering a full winter break halfway through the season. It also ignores the fact that whenever a World Cup is held in a southern hemisphere country, such as Argentina, Chile, Brazil or South Africa, this is in *their* winter, and so disrupts *their* football season!

Much of this is down to a little Englander mentality, best expressed by the then chairman of the Premier League, Sir Dave Richards, at a press conference in Qatar in 2012 (though the Premier League quickly distanced itself from his comments): 'For 50 years, we owned the game, we were the governance of the game.

We wrote the rules and designed the pitches. Then, 50 years later, some guy came along and said you're liars and they actually stole it. It was called FIFA. Fifty years later, another gang came along called UEFA and stole a bit more.'

As World Cups are usually held in June and July, those held in the southern hemisphere are generally not a problem in terms of the temperature, as they are held in winter, while those in the northern hemisphere, held in summer, *can* be. The first World Cup was in July, but as it was in Uruguay, in the southern hemisphere, this was winter. Heat was a problem at the World Cup in Italy in 1934, particularly at the final, where the temperature reached 40°C (104°F), and again in Italy in 1990. In Brazil in 1950 and again in 2014, despite it being winter, temperatures were a problem at some venues, especially those further north, reaching over 30°C (86°F) at some games. The 2014 World Cup, in Brazil, had the first official three-minute cooling breaks, approximately 30 minutes into each half, when temperatures reached 32°C (90°F).

Many venues in Mexico in 1970 and 1986 were problematic, due to temperatures often rising above

35°C (95°F), or high altitude, or even both, and the games being played in the heat of the early afternoon to suit the television audiences in western Europe. The World Cup in the USA in 1994 had high temperature and humidity problems. At one game the temperature reached 45°C (113°F)! The vast majority of games were again played in the early afternoon to accommodate European television. Italy's captain, Franco Baresi, said, 'We are preparing to suffer.' Brazil defender Leonardo said, 'This weather could give us an advantage over our opponents, but we would prefer it to be cooler.'

Even in Germany in 1974 and 2006, the temperature was a problem. In 2006 all the afternoon games were quite slow, because of the heat, and the evening games were much more attacking. In 2006 the temperature nearly got the better of David Beckham, who, suffering from dehydration, was sick twice in the second half of England's game against Ecuador. Beckham beat the heat, however, by scoring a trademark free kick to put England through to the quarter-finals.

High temperatures and humidity were an issue in the summer World Cup in Japan and South Korea in

2002. In the quarter-final match, which England lost 2-1 to Brazil, they tired very badly. No wonder. An hour before kick-off, the temperature in the stadium was 28°C (82°F) and the humidity was 57 per cent.

South Africa 2010 was the first winter World Cup since Argentina in 1978 and had the ideal combination of cool temperatures and the ability to have games kicking off at 4:30 p.m. and 8:30 p.m. local time. In Russia in 2018, 25°C (77°F) was the average, and temperatures approached 30°C (86°F) with high humidity at some of the more southerly venues. In 2026, the World Cup is returning to the USA and Mexico – in summer.

What the English in particular are implying is that there should be no World Cups in hot countries in winter, as this disrupts *our* leagues. But this forgets that half the football leagues in the world, those in the southern hemisphere, are played in our summer, their winter. But World Cups in the northern hemisphere in many countries, as we have seen, can be hot and humid in summer, for example, in Italy, the USA, even Germany, and should arguably be played in winter. There is more a case that *all* World Cups should be in the winter rather than summer. There is no FIFA rule as to exactly when a World Cup should be held. It means there are a band of countries around the Equator that many think should never hold a World Cup. But it's the world's game, it belongs to everyone. Why can't we embrace and celebrate this?

41

IT'S *NOT* A GAME OF TWO HALVES

Your team has a poor first half, but you know that means they will be much better in the second. Or your team has played really well in the first half, so you know they won't be able to repeat that, they never do, they are likely to be poor in the second. Why can't they ever play two good halves in a match? How hard can that be? Whatever the score is at half time, you know it can all change – after all, it's a game of two halves, isn't it? The problem is, by and large it isn't, at least in terms of results.

In Premier League history, the half time score – win, lose or draw – has been unchanged at the final whistle in 60 per cent of matches. The one thing you are more likely to see in the second half is goals – slightly. Despite the fact that results are less likely to change during the second period, it's 25 per cent more likely that a goal is scored after the break. In Premier League history, 44 per cent of goals have been scored during the first half and 56 per cent in the second. This is the same in every major league in the world. But still 6 times out of 10 the half time score position does not change.

Why is this? It's because football is such a low-scoring sport, compared with most others. This means that it is comparatively unlikely for a half time score position to change. There is an invaluable study of all the English Football League results from the beginning in 1888 to 2014 – that's 186,060 matches. The average number of goals per game has declined since 1888, as teams have become tactically more astute in defence. It's down from an average of 4.5 goals per game in the 1880s to about 2.66 today. Indeed, the history of soccer formations demonstrates this, moving from 1-1-8 at the start (1 defender, 1 midfielder, 8 attackers), to 2-3-5, 4-2-4, 4-3-3, 4-4-2, 4-5-1, to even 4-6-0 today. In 1888–89, only 17 per cent of games were drawn; now it's around 26 per cent, as goals go down and results become tighter. In 85,694 matches – almost half – one of the teams has failed to score. So if you follow your team home and away, in a quarter of games they are likely to fail to score at all! The most common results have been 1-0 (16 per cent of matches), 0-0 (14 per cent – there have been over 13,000 0-0 draws!), 2-1 (14 per cent), 2-0 (11 per cent), 1-1 (11 per cent). So two-thirds of matches finish with one of these scores: 0-0, 1-0, 0-1, 2-1, 1-2, 2-0 or 0-2.

With these likely outcomes, the most likely scores at half time are 0-0, 1-0 and 0-1. This means that while there are likely to be slightly more goals on average in the second half, the results are much less likely to change. Most often, it's *not* a game of two halves!

42

WEMBLEY IS *NOT* A WORLD-CLASS STADIUM, AND NEVER HAS BEEN

The original Wembley Stadium, or the British Empire Exhibition Stadium to give it its proper title, was built as part of the British Empire Exhibition of 1924 and 1925, at a cost of £750,000. It was originally intended that the stadium would be demolished at the end of the exhibition, along with all the other buildings.

The stadium was completed in April 1923 and the FA had seen an opportunity, as a one-off, to have the FA Cup final at a ground that could hold 127,000, which was more than Chelsea's 100,000 capacity Stamford Bridge stadium, which had hosted the three previous FA Cup finals. The FA grossly underestimated the number of people who would come – although in fairness the crowd at the previous year's Cup final had only been 53,000 – so no tickets were issued. The excitement of seeing the new stadium led to up to 300,000 people coming to the game, with at least 60,000 locked outside. This was a near disaster, akin to the Hillsborough disaster of 1989. Fortunately, unlike at Hillsborough, there were no pitch-side fences, and so fans were able to spill out on to, and completely fill, the pitch. However, around 1,000 people were injured, some of them quite seriously. Wembley opened with a near disaster.

A sub-myth is that this became known as the 'White Horse Final', as Billy, the white police horse, cleared the fans from the pitch. But Billy was not white, was in fact called Billie, and was just one of a large number of police horses and police on foot who cleared the pitch so that the game could go ahead. Billie the horse was actually grey, but appeared white in the high-contrast, black-and-white newsreel footage of the era.

Lessons were learned after this near disaster in 1923 and 91,000 people safely attended the Cup Final at Wembley in 1924, but that of 1925 was likely to be the last. At the end of the Empire Exhibition, the entrepreneur Arthur Elvin started buying the derelict buildings one by one, demolishing them and selling the scrap. The stadium had gone into liquidation after it was pronounced 'financially unviable'. Elvin offered to buy the stadium for £127,000 from its owners, Wembley Company, which then immediately bought it back from Elvin, leaving him with a healthy profit. Instead of cash, he received shares, which gave him the largest stake in Wembley Stadium, and he subsequently became chairman. Wembley became a going concern, not through football, which was largely limited to the FA Cup final each year, but through other, much more regular sports, particularly greyhound racing and speedway. England football internationals were held at grounds around the country, with much lower capacities than Wembley, as these could accommodate the anticipated crowds. The only exception was the biannual international against Scotland, which was usually held at Wembley because of the larger crowds that were expected. The first international against a team other than Scotland at Wembley was not until 1951, against Argentina, but even then games were still held elsewhere – just 10 days later, England played Portugal at Goodison Park. Not until the new Wembley opened in 2007 did England start to play all their matches at Wembley, and since 2016 they have again started to play matches at other stadiums in England.

Wembley was undoubtedly an outstanding stadium when it opened in 1923 – though it hadn't been built for football – but as a stadium it was soon overtaken in quality and size by others around the world. In 1930 it was outshone by the Centenary Stadium in Montevideo, built by Uruguay for the first FIFA World Cup. The Maracanã Stadium in Rio de Janeiro, opened to host the World Cup in 1950, was clearly a major advance on Wembley, and could hold 200,000 fans. Despite the English climate, Wembley did not have an all-encircling roof until 1963. Wembley was arguably not even the best stadium in the UK. Hampden Park in Glasgow was the biggest stadium in the world from its opening in 1903 until it was surpassed by the Maracanã in 1950.

By the 1970s and 1980s, Wembley was a seedy stadium with wooden seats and benches, and poor views behind pillars, set in an extremely unappealing industrial estate. It got some new seats and a bit of a makeover for the UEFA Euro '96 tournament, but it needed a major refurbishment. The last England game at the old Wembley stadium was in 2000; it was demolished in 2002–3, but the new Wembley did not open until 2007. The original budget of £458 million spiralled to £798 million. The total cost of the project (including local transport infrastructure redevelopment and the cost of financing) was estimated to be £1 billion. The new Wembley is an extremely underwhelming stadium, compared with others around the world, and even in the UK. It only holds 90,000, and not the 100,000 of major stadiums, due to the need to have an ugly ring of corporate boxes. It is marred by extremely ugly concrete flyovers and walkways outside. It is soulless and second-rate. The FA Cup final at Wembley is no longer the main game of the season, and some are not even sold out. England performed better when they were on the road playing at club stadiums around the country during the construction of the new Wembley between 2001 and 2007, and everyone agreed the atmosphere at these grounds for England games was much better. The new Wembley just shows that we didn't need a national stadium at all.

43

DISABLED PLAYERS ARE *NOT* NEW – THEY HAVE ALWAYS BEEN PART OF THE GAME

Football and disability? What do you think of? A few people in wheelchairs at the side of the pitch at a big stadium. But their carers are holding an umbrella over their heads, because the roof doesn't cover the pitch side from the rain. Or if there is a designated space for wheelchair users, there are never enough spaces, and their view is not great. But of course this is a stereotype, as the vast majority of people with disabilities are not wheelchair users. Disabled supporters are anonymous, and their needs have only come to attention through their own efforts, such as in the UK through lobbying by the National Association of Disabled Supporters, now widened to embrace all sports as the organisation 'Level Playing Field'.

But there have been disabled fans at games since the beginning of the game, and in very large numbers during and immediately after the First World War, when many charity matches were held to raise funds for men from the armed forces who had become disabled through military action in the war. This, after all, is partly how and why women's football became so popular in England during and after the war, with the women playing to raise money for disabled ex-servicemen and their families. In 1917, as a fundraiser, a women's team played against a team of ex-servicemen that included men who had lost arms in the war. The other male players had their arms tied behind their backs. Football became part of the therapy for the recovery of many disabled servicemen in the First World War, especially those who had lost their sight. According to the official website of the Paralympic movement, 'Spain are considered the pioneer of blind football, having played the sport since the 1920s', but blind football was being played in England in 1918.

Deaf football has an even longer history. The Glasgow Deaf and Dumb Football Club was the first deaf football club in the world, having been founded in 1871, just eight years after the beginning of Association football! It remains in existence today, as Glasgow Deaf Athletic Football Club. It is one of the oldest football clubs in the world, pre-dating both its illustrious Glasgow neighbours Rangers (1872) and Celtic (1887), and all but five English football league clubs. Deaf football spread significantly across Britain in the late 19th century.

Some top-level footballers have been deaf or partially deaf, such as Cliff Bastin, who was signed by Arsenal in 1929 and with them won the FA Cup twice and the League five times up to 1938. Bastin was Arsenal's highest goal scorer until he was overtaken by Ian Wright in 1997, and still only Wright and Thierry Henry have scored more for Arsenal. Bastin was only 27 at the outbreak of the Second World War in 1939, thus cutting short what should have been the peak of his career. Bastin was excused military service as he failed the army's hearing test owing to his increasing deafness. During the war, he served as an air raid precaution (ARP) warden, stationed on top of Arsenal's Highbury stadium!

Other highly successful footballers have also had significant disabilities. For example, when he was 13, the Uruguayan Héctor Castro accidentally amputated his right forearm while using an electric saw – the origin of his nickname, 'El Manco', meaning 'the one-armed' or 'the maimed', or even, apparently, 'El Divino Manco', 'the one-armed god'. Playing for Uruguay at the 1928 Olympic Games, Castro won a gold medal, scoring in the quarter-final win against Germany. He went on to score the winning goal for Uruguay in the first World Cup Final in 1930.

Other forms of football for people with a range of disabilities have developed in recent years. For example, in the UK there is amputee football, hearing-impaired, learning disability, partially sighted, and wheelchair and power chair football. But it has taken time for all these to get the profile they deserve.

Seven-a-side football has been part of the Paralympic programme since the New York and Stoke Mandeville 1984 Games, when two events were held, one for men with wheelchairs and one for men standing. Every Paralympics since then has consisted of only standing men's team events. Seven-a-side football is played by athletes with cerebral palsy. It follows FIFA rules, with some modifications. Five-a-side football made its Paralympic debut at Athens in 2004. Although athletes may have different degrees of visual impairment, all four outfield players must wear blackout masks to ensure fairness. As yet there is no women's football in the Paralympics, and this needs to change as soon as possible. Yet despite the prejudice and discrimination, disabled players are *not* new – they have always been part of the game.

44

ENGLAND WILL *NEVER* WIN THE WORLD CUP AGAIN

Sorry to say, England fans (and that includes me), but England flattered to deceive at the 2018 World Cup. And they will *never* win it again, unless there is a fundamental change in the English game. The senior men's team, that is. England's women have a good chance of winning the World Cup in the near future. And we may well have further successes to cheer, like when the England men's Under-17 team won the World Cup in India in 2017, after an incredible 5-2 comeback victory over Spain. But the England men's senior team World Cup win in 1966 will not, as things stand, be repeated.

Some will say that England could have won in 2018. I take nothing away from the squad and the manager. In reaching the semi-finals they did very well, exceeding all expectations. But they came up short in the semi-final against Croatia, a team that at that time was 20th in the FIFA rankings, whereas England were 12th. England were expected to get out of their group, but they lost to Belgium, who were clearly a much better side, at that time 3rd in the FIFA rankings. England beat 21st-ranked Tunisia 2-1, but only with an added time goal, and then beat 55th-placed Panama 6-1. In the last 16 game, England, though the better side, only got past 16th-ranked Colombia after extra time and penalties. In the quarter-final, England eased past 24th-ranked Sweden 2-0. So reaching the semi-final was creditable, and an over-achievement.

Indeed, some statisticians have argued that England should not expect to win the World Cup again. Given the size of the population, and the number of registered players we have, getting to the last 16 is what we should aim to do. After that the World Cup is a *cup*, and then anything can happen. But then we look at Germany, which has been in the final eight times, and won it four times, and think, why not us?

It's complicated, but broadly we just don't take it seriously enough. In England, the clubs and the league have always come first. As I have shown elsewhere, English football fans don't really care about the national team, or at least only briefly every two years, if they qualify for the European Championship or the World Cup. With the advent of the Premier League, the national team has become even less significant. All the power is in the hands of the Premier League and the Premier League clubs, not the FA, which runs the England teams. The Premier League is dominated by non-English players; few young English players get the chance to play at the top level. The Premier League needs instant success, and so a manager cannot risk too many, or any, young English players, if he can simply buy the equivalent, finished, experienced version of that player from another country.

But don't take my word for it. In 2015, five former England managers – Glenn Hoddle, Kevin Keegan, Sven-Göran Eriksson, Graham Taylor and Steve McClaren – sent a joint letter to the then FA chairman, Greg Dyke, saying that without fundamental reform, England were unlikely ever to win the World Cup again. The key reason given was the lack of opportunities for young English players to play in the Premier League. The proportion of English players by 2015 was just 32 per cent, down from almost 70 per cent in 1995. They stated that the 'evidence has demonstrated the pool of English talent playing at the very top level is shrinking and it's an undeniable fact that this is a clear disadvantage for any England manager'. In May 2019 England manager Gareth Southgate warned that within a decade this figure could be down to just 15 per cent, which would be 'a big danger for us'.

It's all about money. The Premier League, its clubs and players, take most of it. The FA has relatively little to invest in grass-roots football, and we have a major problem with poor facilities, largely as a result, and declining playing rates among men and boys, which is also connected. England's St George's Park National Football Centre, opened in 2012, is a very positive development, but it's an oasis in a desert. This is unlike many other – successful – European countries, such as Germany, the Netherlands, Belgium and Spain, where the FA has kept the power, kept a lot of the money, and invested it in the grass roots. It comes to something when the biggest potential step forward financially for grass-roots football is when the FA gets an offer to sell its national stadium – Wembley.

As long as the Premier League has the power and the money, any change in the fortunes of the England men's team will be superficial. Only root and branch reform of the FA and its relationship with the Premier League can change things. There is no sign that this will happen. And so England's men will never win the World Cup again.

45

FOOTBALL IN INDIA IS *NOT* NEW – AND HAS A GREATER TRADITION THAN CRICKET

When those outside India think about sport in that country, we automatically think of cricket. But this is an outsider's perspective, from the present day. Football in India is not new, and has a greater tradition than cricket.

Historically, India had many of its own sports, one of which, kabaddi, is having a major resurgence through national and international TV coverage. The first Western sport that India excelled at was hockey (in some countries termed field hockey). It's still very popular among Indian men and women. The Indian men's team first competed in the 1928 Olympics, long before independence from the British, winning gold. They also won gold at the next five Olympics, and eight golds in total up to 1980.

Cricket, by comparison, was historically a smaller sport in terms of the number of players, and didn't gain mass popularity until after the Indian cricket team started to perform well. India made its Test Cricket debut in 1932, but didn't win a test until 1952. Decades of steady improvement followed, but the game only really took off in the national public imagination when India won the Cricket World Cup in 1983, defeating the favourites and two-time defending champions the West Indies in the final. At that time, the West Indies were the best cricket team in the world. Sachin Tendulkar joined the test team in 1989 and became India's first cricket superstar. India's international results have continued to improve. In 2008, the launch of the Twenty20 cricket league, the Indian Premier League, drawing star players from around the world, took cricket in India to a new level, both in terms of attendances at games and mass TV audiences. Cricket is now huge in India, but it is relatively recent, since the 1990s.

So what of football? The British brought the game as the imperial rulers of India and spread it principally through the British Army stationed in the country. The Durand Cup, first held in Shimla in 1888, was the first Indian competition and is the third oldest surviving football competition in the world, after the English and Scottish FA Cups. The Indians soon took up the game and in 1892 the Sovabazar Club, in beating the East Surrey Regiment, became the first Indian team to beat a British side. The first of India's major clubs, which is still going today, was Mohun Bagan. They made history in 1911 by becoming the first Indian team to win a major trophy, the Indian Football Association Shield, beating the East Yorkshire Regiment in the final, in front of 60,000 fans. This became part of the narrative of the independence movement. If they could even beat the British at their own game – football – why shouldn't they run their own country? Mahatma Gandhi started two football clubs during his time in South Africa, both named the Passive Resisters, challenging racial discrimination and injustice through non-violent resistance.

Football drew huge crowds and had mass popularity in some parts of India, especially in Bengal. Indian teams started to play overseas from the 1930s, including internationals. The All India Football Federation was founded in 1937. After independence, a barefooted Indian team played at the 1948 Olympics, losing only 2-1 to France, after missing two penalties. India did not refuse to go to the World Cup in Brazil in 1950 because FIFA had banned them from playing barefoot – this is a myth. They would have played in boots, but chose not to go in part because of the cost of travel, and also because at the time they favoured the Olympics over the World Cup. As we have seen, at this time the Olympics was still widely regarded as the leading international football competition, rather than the FIFA World Cup. In the 1950s India became the best team in Asia, performed well at Olympic football tournaments and won the Asian Games. The game also remained very popular in many regions of the country.

India is a vast country, and until recently a rather poor one. Despite large crowds, football facilities were relatively poor, and there was no national league until 1996. Football was regionalised, very popular in some places, largely unknown in others. But the same, to some extent, can also be said of cricket in India. Football in India has a long and strong history, but it's been relatively weak in performance, especially in international terms, for the last few decades. India is currently ranked 101st (as of June 2019) by FIFA, and has been much lower. This doesn't inspire the next generation, when the cricket team is often ranked number one, and there is big money to be made in cricket, but not football. But this is changing. TV has brought the football leagues of Europe to India, and the English Premier League and

La Liga have proved immensely popular. Now there are two successful competing professional leagues in India. There was untapped interest; India was a sleeping giant in terms of football. Crucially, some of the teams are backed, and part-owned, by some of the biggest names in Indian cricket, such as Tendulkar, Sourav Ganguly and Virat Kohli. Gates are very strong and TV audiences have become large very quickly, even rivalling the Indian Premier League cricket. Football has not come from nowhere in India, whereas arguably cricket did. Football in India has long, deep roots. Football in the past was more popular than cricket in India – and today, it is beginning to rival cricket once more.

46

THE ZAIRE PLAYER IN *THAT* WORLD CUP MOMENT *DID* KNOW THE RULES – HE WAS IN FEAR OF HIS LIFE

The World Cup in West Germany, 1974. Brazil versus Zaire. A free kick to Brazil on the edge of the Zaire box. Rivelino is about to unleash one of his trademark free kicks. But before the referee can blow his whistle, a Zaire player comes out of the wall and boots the ball away into the Brazilian half. One of the weirdest ever World Cup moments. An act of total madness? Did the Zaire player not understand the rules? This is what we have come to believe. But of course he knew the rules. He knew exactly what he was doing. And he even feared his life might depend on it.

In 1974, the football team of Zaire (now the Democratic Republic of the Congo) was on a real high. In March they won the African Cup of Nations in Egypt, and had qualified for the 1974 World Cup in West Germany, having beaten Morocco, the African team that had competed in 1970. In doing so, Zaire became the first sub-Saharan African team to participate at a World Cup. The country's dictator, President Mobutu, was strongly backing the team. Indeed, he paid for advertising hoardings at the World Cup to display messages such as 'Zaire – Peace' and 'Go to Zaire'. Mobutu had gained power in a CIA-backed coup in 1965 and he saw football as an excellent publicity opportunity for his country. In 1974 he would organise and host the famous 'Rumble in the Jungle' world heavyweight boxing fight between Muhammad Ali and George Foreman. Mobutu even had a hand in the design of the team's shirts for Germany – 'yellow, to look like 11 Pelés' – with a large leopard's head on the front.

In the build-up, Mobutu banned players from Zaire playing abroad, even though many were good enough. He did not want them to become 'mercenaries' in Europe, like many other African footballers who already were. The downside, of course, was that they did not gain the experience of playing in European leagues, against Europeans. Despite lavish praise and extravagant promises of gifts from Mobutu, the team feared his reaction if they did not perform well at the World Cup.

In Germany, Zaire began with a creditable 2-0 defeat to Scotland, who themselves rather unluckily later went out of the tournament unbeaten, on goal difference, after drawing with Brazil and Yugoslavia. A rude awakening for the Zaire team was the racist abuse meted out to them by one of the Scottish players in particular. Zaire did not fare so well in their next game, losing 9-0 to Yugoslavia. Before the game the players became concerned that they weren't going to receive promised payments, and threatened not to play. This was far from ideal preparation, and they started the game very badly, going 3-0 down after 18 minutes. Bizarrely, their Yugoslavian coach Vidinic then substituted the highly experienced first choice keeper Kazadi Mwamba, who had had a good game against Scotland, with Tubilandu Ndimbi. This was the first time in a World Cup that a keeper had been substituted for any reason other than injury. Asked afterwards why he did this, Vidinic said it was a 'state secret', fuelling rumours that government officials had intervened, as Ndimbi was said to have friends in 'high places'. After 22 minutes Zaire were also down to ten men. After this defeat (still a World Cup finals record), Mobutu sent them a message: 'You're scum and sons of whores … if you concede more than three against Brazil in the final match, you will never see Zaire or your families again.'

It was in the 78th minute of Zaire's last group game, against Brazil, that one of the most bizarre moments in World Cup history happened. Indeed, this was voted the 17th greatest World Cup moment in a British TV (Channel 4) poll. With Brazil leading 2-0, the Brazilian free-kick specialist Rivelino was ready to take a kick from just outside the penalty area. Brazil needed to win 3-0 to be sure to qualify from the group on goal difference ahead of Scotland. Before the referee blew his whistle, the Zaire player Mwepu Ilunga came out of the defensive wall and kicked the ball away. At the time, British journalists and pundits put this down to 'naivety', with more than a hint of racism in their reaction. BBC TV's Barry Davies, commenting live on the game, said: 'What on earth did he do that for? … a bizarre moment of African innocence.' Ilunga received a yellow card from the bemused referee. According to one report, Ilunga stated that he was quite aware of the rules and was hoping to convince the referee to send him off. The intended red card would have been a protest against his country's authorities, who were allegedly depriving the players of their earnings.

In reality, Ilunga kicked the ball away for fear of going 3-0 down with so much time left in the match. He was aiming to waste some vital time. Rivelino's kick hit the wall and Ilunga hoofed it away legitimately. However, Brazil scored just a minute later. Zaire lost only 3-0, a creditable result against the then World Champions Brazil. Contrary to rumours, Mobutu did not have some of the players killed. He withdrew funding from the national team, which was eliminated in the first round of the African Nations Cup in 1976, did not qualify for the tournament from 1978 to 1986, did not participate in qualification for the 1978 FIFA World Cup, and has failed to qualify for the World Cup Finals ever since. Most of the players subsequently lived in poverty, apparently still banned from seeking contracts in Europe. Ndaye Mulamba, arguably the most talented player in the team, ended up begging on the streets of Cape Town. A tragic waste of a highly talented group of players.

47

THERE *ARE* GREAT FOOTBALL FILMS

Football fans agree that there are no great football films. The view is that film cannot capture the essence of the live game. When films recreate action on the pitch, it often seems wrong, and this seems to devalue the whole experience. But by this measure there would be no great sports films. Or war films for that matter, because how can they recreate the action on the battlefield? But this misunderstands what films are for. They are not re-creations. A football film does not seek to recreate a live football match. Football isn't just about 90 minutes on the pitch. It's 24 hours a day, 365 days a year, it's about events behind the scenes, the media, the fans. Just as a war film isn't just about the battlefield. A football film is either a documentary or a piece of fiction that explores an aspect or aspects of the game, usually through a group of characters. Yet football films like *Escape to Victory* are tolerated but viewed ironically, as in 'it's not very good really, though is it?', a kind of guilty pleasure that we shouldn't be caught watching. But there are many great football films – and *Escape to Victory* is one of them.

Football films, both documentaries and fiction, have a long pedigree. The first football film dates from 1896, demonstrating the social significance of this new sport of Association football; it is about 90 seconds of a match between Blackburn Rovers and West Bromwich Albion. Blackburn-based film-makers Mitchell and Kenyon then produced scores of football films in England prior to the First World War, which had match action, but – fascinatingly – crowd footage too, as the commercial value was in the fans paying to come and see themselves in the film that evening! The first dramatic silent football film dates from 1911. Of particular note from the inter-war period is *The Arsenal Stadium Mystery*, a detective story set at Arsenal's Highbury stadium, and featuring the Arsenal team, which was then the leading side in the country.

Since the 1940s there have been a large number of cinema and television films seeking to exploit football's popularity. Some are of dubious quality, but some are quite outstanding, by film-makers of international repute. *Goal!,* the official FIFA film of the 1966 World Cup, is a fabulous documentary record of the tournament, and of England as a country in 1966. Ken Loach's *The*

Golden Vision (1968) is about a group of Everton fans who miss births, weddings and funerals to see their team play. Ken Loach's *Kes* (1969) has one of the best football sequences in a non-football film. Jack Rosenthal wrote and Michael Apted directed the wonderful *Another Sunday and Sweet FA* (1972), set during just one game. *Escape to Victory* (1981), directed by Hollywood legend John Huston and starring, among others, Pelé, Michael Caine and Sylvester Stallone, is an inspirational story. If football fans don't rate it, why do they always watch it when it's on TV every Christmas? *Gregory's Girl*, also from 1981, is a wonderful football-based comedy, which puts a female footballer at the heart of the action, and pre-dates *Bend It Like Beckham* by over 20 years. *The Cup* (1999) is a Tibetan-language film directed by Khyentse Norbu, which shows the desperate lengths to which young football-crazed Tibetan refugee novice Buddhist monks in a remote Himalayan monastery in India go to obtain a television for the monastery in order to watch the 1998 World Cup Final. If any film best shows the universal power of football, this is it! The *Goal!* series of films, beginning in 2005, are very realistic in terms of the football action, and very popular with fans as a result, though the plots are rather clichéd. For a dramatised piece of history there is *The Miracle of Bern*, West Germany's triumph in the 1954 World Cup Final. In most football films the game is about belonging and solidarity, but Iranian director Jafar Panahi's *Offside* (2006) focuses on exclusion, as a group of young women attempt to get into the men-only stadium to see Iran's crucial World Cup qualifier against Bahrain. Ken Loach returned to a football theme with the very wonderful *Looking for Eric* (2009), featuring Eric Cantona as himself. *The Damned United* (2009) is a fascinating portrayal of English manager Brian Clough. *United* (2011) is a harrowing dramatisation of Manchester United's Munich air disaster in 1958. For me, the funniest football films are *Mike Bassett: England Manager*, about an archetypal England international team coach, which is probably only funny if you are a long-suffering England football fan, and *Männer wie wir* (*Men like us*), ludicrously called *Guys and Balls* in English, a German film about a gay man who suffers homophobic abuse in his current team, so forms an all-gay team to seek revenge.

Not yet convinced? Then I will add my two favourite football documentaries. *The Other Final* is a 2003 film about football matches, home and away, between Bhutan and Montserrat, the then lowest-ranked teams in the FIFA World Rankings, which shows how two completely different cultures, from other sides of the world, came together beautifully through football. *Next Goal Wins* is a fascinating and very moving 2014 British documentary film that follows American Samoa's national football team, derided as one of the poorest teams in the world after a 31-0 defeat to Australia, as they attempt to regain their self-belief and reputation, and qualify for the 2014 World Cup under the guidance of an inspirational Dutch coach. No great football films? I know there are. I have seen them. And there will be many more to come…

48

THE PREMIER LEAGUE IS *NOT* EXCITING – IT'S INCREASINGLY DULL AND PREDICTABLE

If you believed the hype, you would think the Premier League is the most exciting sports competition on the planet. But it's not. It's not exciting, and it's increasingly dull and predictable. Sure, there are some great players on show, and some great matches. There are in many top leagues. But despite all the money, the Premier League fails to attract the very best of the world's players at the height of their powers.

However, the problem with the Premier League is much deeper than this. It's increasingly uncompetitive. We know at the beginning of each season which teams will almost certainly finish in the top six, and increasingly even the top four. We have a pretty good idea who will even win it. The rest will be battling to stay up. Indeed, the most exciting part of the Premier League season now is the fight to avoid relegation. We know what's likely to happen before it's happened, which kills the magical unpredictability of sport. Statistically, the richest clubs, those who can spend the most on players' wages, will finish higher. The likely finishing positions of the League can be predicted before the start of the season with great accuracy, based on the wages each can afford to pay. Leicester City's win was a brief, probably last, flicker of magic. Unless there is a revolutionary change to the Premier League, of which there is no sign.

The Premier League is losing what is termed 'competitive balance', the situation in which no one business of a group of competing businesses has an unfair advantage over the others. In the 21 seasons of the old First Division, the then top flight of English football, which became the Premier League, between 1971–72 and 1991–92, there were seven different champions: Liverpool and Arsenal, but also Everton, Aston Villa, Leeds United, Nottingham Forest and Derby County. Note there was no Manchester United, Manchester City, Chelsea or Spurs. Eighteen different teams finished in the top three. It wasn't perfect, but it wasn't predictable.

Compare this with the 27 seasons of the Premier League to date. There have been just six different winners: Manchester United, Manchester City, Arsenal, Chelsea, Leicester City and Blackburn Rovers. Blackburn's win was back in 1995 and they are now in the Championship, having gone down even to League One for a season. Only 13 different teams have finished in the top three, and only seven teams in the top three since 2002–03. Only 14 teams have ever finished in the top four of the Premier League. This is increasingly predictable.

In contrast, major sports in the USA, such as baseball, basketball and American football, realise that it is very important to have competitive balance. Despite whatever happened last season, fans need to know there is a chance that their team could not only do much better this season, but could even be the champions. And it happens. Take the NFL. In the same period as the Premier League to date, that is, since 1993, there have been a staggering 22 different finalists in the Super Bowl, and 14 different winners. It's exciting and unpredictable; every team has a chance each season. By comparison, the Premier League has had just nine teams finish second and six different winners in that time. American sports have a number of different ways of protecting competitive balance, including salary caps and revenue sharing. They know how vital it is to the long-term appeal and success of their sports.

The danger for the Premier League is that the growing gulf in wealth between the top six and the rest will become increasingly entrenched, and make the league increasingly predictable, turning off fans and TV viewers. As Mervyn King, the former governor of the Bank of England and a director at Aston Villa, has said: 'The Premier League should be worried that global fans just want to watch the top three or four teams rather than the whole league.' The fear is that globalisation is helping the Premier League's 'big six' become as entrenched as big technology's 'big five' – Amazon, Google, Apple, Microsoft and Facebook – making it impossible for the competition to catch up. The Premier League is becoming increasingly predictable, and therefore increasingly less exciting.

49

SIR ALEX FERGUSON IS *NOT* THE GREATEST EVER MANAGER IN ENGLISH FOOTBALL

Ask fans who has been the most successful manager of all time in English football and most will probably say Sir Alex Ferguson. No one comes close to 13 Premier League titles, five FA Cups, four League Cups, one UEFA Cup Winners' Cup and two UEFA Champions League wins. However, Liverpool fans will quite rightly point to Bob Paisley's magnificent record of six League titles, three League Cups, one UEFA Cup and three European Cups in just nine seasons. Ferguson, by contrast, was United's manager for 27 seasons. Ask who is the greatest manager of all time, and perhaps a majority will also say Sir Alex. However, and partly depending on the age of the person and how much they know of football history, you might get a range of other answers, including Herbert Chapman, Sir Matt Busby, Bill Shankly, Bob Paisley, Don Revie and Sir Alf Ramsey, for winning the World Cup in 1966. Many would also say Brian Clough. And they would be right. Rather than Sir Alex Ferguson or Bob Paisley,

Brian Clough (with Peter Taylor) is the greatest ever manager in English football history.

In May 1967, after a managerial apprenticeship at Hartlepool United, Brian Clough and Peter Taylor joined Second Division side Derby County as manager and assistant manager. Derby County had just finished 17th in the table, and had been a very average Second Division team for over 10 years. The only major trophy the club had ever won was the FA Cup in 1946. In 1967–68 Derby won the Second Division title, and in 1971–72 they won the First Division title for the first time. In 1972–73 they reached the semi-final of the European Cup. All this was achieved on a relatively tight budget and without big star-name players. Clough and Taylor left in October 1973 after falling out with the chairman. The following season, with Clough and Taylor's team, new manager Dave Mackay won Derby's second First Division title, but the club has won no major honours since, and has spent most of the time since then outside the top flight of English football.

Clough and Taylor then had an unsuccessful spell at Brighton, in the Third Division, but Clough was there less than a year before he went to top-flight Leeds

United, where he lasted only 44 days before he was sacked. Clough became Nottingham Forest manager in 1975. Forest were a very average Second Division side, and their only previous honours were FA Cup wins in 1898 and 1959. Taylor rejoined Clough as his assistant manager for the start of the 1976–77 season, and at the end of it Forest were promoted to the First Division. Taylor's knack of signing players no one else seemed to rate, together with Clough's charismatic leadership, took Forest to unparalleled success. Following this promotion, Forest won the First Division title for the first time in their history, finishing seven points clear of a great Liverpool side, also beating Liverpool to win the League Cup. The following season, Forest finished second in the League, to Liverpool, but won the League Cup and, extraordinarily, the European Cup. The following season they won the European Cup again.

Forest never achieved such success again. Some point to Taylor's retirement in 1982, saying that Clough could not achieve success without Taylor. But this is simplistic. Forest was a club of relatively limited financial resources and it had massively over-achieved through inspirational management. Under Clough, Forest continued to achieve far more than a club of its size would be expected to, competing in the top flight. There were two League Cup wins, and Forest were cheated in being beaten by Anderlecht in the 1983–84 UEFA Cup semi-final, as 10 years later it was proven the referee had been bribed by Anderlecht's chairman. Clough couldn't repeat the success, not just because he didn't have Taylor with him, or was increasingly battling alcoholism. This is to take away from Clough's achievements at Forest in this era. Forest were still punching way above their weight. They could not compete with the top clubs for players' wages. Clough couldn't afford to keep England goalkeeper Peter Shilton as early as 1982, as Shilton was offered higher wages at Southampton. As Clough later joked, 'We even offered him the Main Stand to stay.' Forest are now back at the level one might expect them to be in terms of their financial resources. They have been outside the Premier League since 1999, and have even dropped down to the third tier of English football. Clough, with Taylor, at Derby County and then Nottingham Forest, performed the greatest English football miracle – twice.

50
ASSOCIATION FOOTBALL
WILL *NOT* LAST FOREVER

The history of sport shows that no sport lasts forever. Civilisations die, sports die – often together. The ancient Olympic Games in Greece were held from around 776 BC to 393 AD. The Roman sports of the Colosseum died, as the Roman Empire became Christian. In England, cockfighting was one of the major sports until 1835, when it was banned – though it continued illegally. Sports also metamorphose as values change. Sport in Victorian England tended to mean the hunting of animals, but many of these are now not deemed appropriate. Hare coursing was changed into the 'civilised' sport of greyhound racing. As with all things, sports are born, develop and die. This is probably inevitable. It is ridiculous arrogance to think that Association football will be any different. After all, it's only been around for just over 150 years!

There were of course many forms of football games around the world before the English FA created the laws of Association football in 1863. But those standardising these rules in 1863 didn't do this to establish a global sport. Indeed, the reason it is called simply the Football Association, rather than the English Football Association, was that the founders of the FA had no pretentions that their game would spread even across England – they were not aiming to be national. They simply wanted a common set of agreed laws so that clubs in the FA, in the London area, could play each other, without arguing over the laws. Indeed, the FA saw its role as not to promote the game, but simply to establish a common set of laws. It nearly voted to disband itself after a few years, on the grounds that its mission had been completed. When the Scots founded their own FA in 1873, the name, to distinguish itself, had to be the Scottish Football Association. Every national FA founded since then has the name of the country within it.

Association football did not become and has never been the only form of football in England. From 1871 there was rugby union, and from 1895, rugby league. As we have seen, rugby could have become England's national sport, and rugby league and rugby union are still the main sports in many towns and cities in England. Cricket remained England's national sport until at least 1900. There was no inevitability in the rise of Association football; there is no inevitability in its continued growth, or even survival.

New sports are developing all the time, and some of these are new versions of football, like futsal. Video gaming is now a major sport, with huge arena and online audiences, including football video games. Maybe Association football will get replaced by video gaming. Or, like cuju, it could become more a demonstration of individual skills, and so metamorphose into freestyle football (which already exists), simply clever tricks with the ball, a sophisticated version of 'keepy-uppy'. In 50 years' time, we may see any sport that has any physical contact at all, including even Association football, as 'uncivilised'. Who knows? But Association football *will* come to an end.

ACKNOWLEDGEMENTS

Many thanks to Matthew Lowing from Bloomsbury, whose idea this book was, who commissioned me to write it, and who has guided me superbly throughout. A big thank you also to Sarah Skipper for being an excellent editor, and to Jenni Davis and Lisa Hughes for their great work in copy-editing.

Thanks also to all the National Football Museum staff, historians, museum visitors and others with a passion for the game, who have shared their stories with me – even if some of them weren't true! In writing this, I drew upon a great deal of outstanding research by academic historians of the game in particular, and have listed some of their key books in the bibliography.

I would like to thank those nearest to me who have had to put up with my usual over-enthusiasm mixed with grumpiness while writing a book! Those are my wife Nina, my daughter Zoë and my son Oskar. Thank you for your patience and understanding!

My love of the game came from my family – my grandfather Neill, my father Bob, and my uncles Bryan and Mick. This book is dedicated to the memory of Neill and Bob, and two very special friends, Jane Carney (Bolton Wanderers) and Magnus Larsen (Newcastle United).

AFTERWORD

In debunking these myths, I am sure that I have surprised, entertained, informed, but possibly also annoyed you! None of us like to have our long-cherished beliefs challenged. It pained me to discover, for example, how England's 1966 win was tarnished, that the English didn't spread football in Brazil, and that cheating has always been part of English football. However, I am delighted that black players are not new in the English game, that football hooliganism is not the 'English disease', and that the Germans do not always win on penalties! Football never ceases to amaze me, and finding out that much of what we think we know about it turns out to be a myth makes the game even more fascinating. Myths are powerful, and we also need to try to understand how they develop, and why we want them to be true. Football, warts and all, remains a fantastic game, to play, to watch, and to endlessly debate...

While each myth stands in its own right, there are a couple of themes which emerge. First, that the English tend to have an Anglocentric view of football, past and present. We fail to recognise just how quickly the Scots, Welsh and Irish became a key part of the game, and also how rapidly it spread from the British Isles, not just to Europe, but to every continent – before 1900! Second, while it was initially established as a game for white, upper- and middle-class English men, they were powerless to prevent the game from very rapidly spreading to the working class, women, people with disabilities, black, Asian and minority ethnic groups, and the LGBT community – around the world. This is not to say that white, elite social class men don't still largely control the game, or that they haven't tried to stop these 'others' from joining it. But football is increasingly, very positively, inclusive. The game belongs to all of us…

BIBLIOGRAPHY

I have used a huge range of sources in the research for this book. If I included them all below, this would be hundreds of references. Instead, I have picked a selection of some of the most useful works.

Alegi, Peter, 2010, *African Soccerscapes: How A Continent Changed the World's Game*, Ohio University Press.

Anderson, Chris, Sally, David, 2014, *The Numbers Game: Why Everything You Know About Football is Wrong*, Penguin.

Bandyopadhyay, Kausik, Majumdar, Boria, 2006, *A Social History of Indian Football: Striving to Score*, Routledge.

Carter, Neil, 2006, *The Football Manager*, Routledge.

Collins, Tony, 2013, *Sport in Capitalist Society: A Short History*, Routledge.

Collins, Tony, 2015, *The Oval World: A Global History of Rugby*, Bloomsbury Sport.

Collins, Tony, 2018, *How Football Began: A Global History of How the World's Football Codes Were Born*, Routledge.

Cox, Richard, Vamplew, Wray, Russell, Dave, (eds), 2002, *Encyclopedia of British Football*, Routledge.

Fabian, A.H., Green, Geoffrey, 1960, *Association Football*, Volumes 1–4, Caxton.

Galeano, Eduardo, 2018, *Soccer in Sun and Shadow*, Penguin Modern Classics.

Glanville, Brian, 2011, *The Story of the World Cup*, Faber and Faber.

Goldblatt, David, 2007, *The Ball is Round: A Global History of Soccer*, Penguin.

Hughson, John, 2016, *England and the 1966 World Cup: A Cultural History,* Manchester University Press.

Hughson, John, Moore, Kevin, Maguire, Joseph, Spaaj, Ramon, (eds), 2017, *Routledge Handbook of Football Studies*, Routledge.

Inglis, Simon, 1985, *Soccer in the Dock: A History of British Football Scandals 1900 to 1965*, Willow Books.

Kuper, Simon, Szymanski, Stefan, 2018, *Soccernomics*, Harper Collins.

Lanfranchi, Pierre, Eisenberg, Christiane, Mason, Tony, Wahl, Alfred, 2004, *100 Years of Football: The FIFA Centennial Book*, Wiedenfeld and Nicolson.

Lopez, Sue, 1997, *Women on the Ball: A Guide to Women's Football*, Scarlet Press.

Meisl, Willy, 1956, *Soccer Revolution*, The Sportsmans Book Club.

Menary, Steve, 2010, *GB United? British Olympic Football and the End of the Amateur Dream*, Pitch Publishing.

Moore, Kevin, 2014, 'Football in the Olympic and Paralympics', *Sport in Society*: *special issue – The Olympic Games: Meeting New Global Challenges*: 1–16.

Moore, Kevin, 2016, 'A second "Maracanãzo"? The 2014 FIFA World Cup in historical perspective', *Sport in Society*: 555–571.

Morris, Desmond, 1981, *The Soccer Tribe*, Cape.

Murray, Bill, 1998, *The World's Game: A History of Soccer*, University of Illinois Press.

Reilly, Thomas, 1996, *Science and Soccer*, Chapman and Hall.

Russell, Dave, *Football and the English*: *A Social History of Association Football in England, 1863–1995*, Carnegie.

Simons, Rowan, 2008, *Bamboo Goalposts: One Man's Quest to Teach the People's Republic of China to Love Football*, Pan Macmillan.

Spurling, Jon, 2010, *Death or Glory: The Dark History of the World Cup*, Vision Sports Publishing.

Taylor, Matthew, 2005, *Leaguers: The Making of Professional Football in England, 1900–1939*, Liverpool University Press.

Taylor, Matthew, 2008, *The Association Game: A History of British Football*, Pearson Education.

Taylor, Matthew, 2011, *Football: A Short History*, Shire Library.

Walvin, James, 2000, *The People's Game: The History of Football Revisited*, Mainstream Sport.

Williams, Jean, 2003, *A Game for Rough Girls? A History of Women's Football in England*, Routledge.

Williams, Jean, 2007, *A Beautiful Game: International Perspectives On Women's Football*, Berg.